IS GOD A TRINITY.

BY

REV. JOHN MILLER.

THIRD EDITION.

PRINCETON, N. J.
PRIVATELY PRINTED
1922

PREFACE.

THE author of this book has no other occupation for the remainder of his life one tenth part as interesting to him, as the undoing, as far as his feeble efforts can, prevalent superstitions of the church in respect to the justification of believers.

He finds piety in the Roman Catholic Church, but desperately marred by superstitious additions. So of the Baptist Church; so of the Methodist; so of the ritualistic Episcopalians: a great many good works, and a great many pious experiences, increasing in excellence and amount as the church becomes not Papist but Protestant, and not Protestant alone but down nearer the rock-bed of absolute Christianity.

But this he notices: Churches flourish numerically by force of their superstitions. I offer shares on Wall Street. I get the most bids if there be an element of gambling. If what I have to propose involves hard work, men bid slowly. If it have a speculative cast, men crowd upon me and buy. And so of the different denominations. There are pious people in every one of them. There are the most pious people in those that have most of Christ. But how obvious is it that the children of this world are wiser than the children of light ; and, therefore, that the way-making property of a church, or that by which it gathers numbers, is not the pious points in it, but the superstitions ; or, in other words, the pious points give it character and favor with heaven, but its superstitions cut its way, and load on it its numerical strength, though they bring it at last to its ghostly dissolution.

Let me illustrate this. The Baptists are a pious sect, but who does not see that they make their way by immersion? The Jansenists were an excellent people : and who that has seen much of ritualism is narrow enough to deny, that there are singular instances of faith under the most direful idolatry ? And, yet, it is the idolatry that fights the battle. It is the labor-saving principle. Or rather, it is that which does without purity of life. And, therefore, though good men get into such systems, they are flocked into by the bad : and the ritualism is the speculative cast that makes the sect attractive as in the Wall Street overtures.

Now take our Presbyterian communion. I have thought it the very soberest. It seems down at the hard-pan of actual revelation. What could be more plain ? And, yet, watch its operations. Regard its scenes of present revival. What does it harp upon most? Precisely those things that are capable of superstition.

We have nothing to make a superstition of, ritualistically ; nor in our forms; nor in our measures We have no idols that can be set up, and looked at, unless the eucharist and the sacramental baptism still have cleaving to them, specially in our symbols (Conf. C. 28, § 6; see also Sh. Cat. Qu. 92), a little of the rust of the middle age. We are shut up, like the culprit in a prison, with nothing to commit suicide with, except the bare walls, or the strips we can tear from our covering. And yet the Wall Street appetite is there. How do we gratify it? By seizing that which can be best exsiccated and made insignificant. Our Saviour says, " Repent." It is hard to get facility out of that. Isaiah says, " Wash you: make you clean" (Is. i: 16). Our Lord says, " If thou wilt enter into life, keep the commandments" (Matt. xix: 17). Ezekiel says, " Make you a new heart" (Ez. xviii: 31). The apostle speaks of repentance and conversion for the remission of sin (Acts iii: 19; Mar. i: 4). These are not easy instruments of superstition. And, therefore, faith, which is unspeakably more shadowy, attracts the eager instinct of our humanity as that through which can be made more facile the offerings of salvation.

Now, to a discerning eye, faith and repentance are co-essential: obedience and believing are the same *in nuce*: when our King says, Do well and be accepted (Gen. iv: 7), it is not necessary to have in eye the covenant of works, but repenting and converting. If any man says, We cannot obey perfectly, such a creed echoes, Nor believe perfectly. The true mind looks from Christ to James; and where Christ says, Do my sayings, and thou hast thy house upon a rock (Matt. vii: 24), it asks what those sayings are, and, finding them to teach truth (v: 33–37), and love (v: 44), and meekness (v: 5), and long suffering (v : 39), and honesty (vii : 12), and the commonest duties among men (vii : 1), it understands what the old nation ought to have understood when it was commanded, "Do this and thou shalt live" (Lev. xviii : 5 ; Lu. x : 28); and it reconciles Paul with James when Paul says, A man is justified by faith, if James really had said (see *Auth. Com. on Rom.*), "Ye see, then, how that by works a man is justified, and not by faith only" (Jas. ii : 24).

Now, believing that hypocrites abound; and believing that there are profligates in the church ; and believing that they come there under the hands of ministers ; and hearing these ministers preach ; and believing that they misapprehend the doctrine of salvation,—we would like to spend our life in earnest remonstrance. What the water is to one ; and what the priest is to another ; and what systematical conceits of order may be to the salvation of a third; that, I believe, mere trust, without a particle of moral trait, is to the everlasting salvation of many of our people.

Now, unfortunately to the outward eye, in this zeal for purity of life, this would-be reformation of my brethren, finds itself confronted with another faith, which, it is to be feared, will cast, oceans of distance from me, the purest of the people.

Why write about it?

This is the very point that is pressed by almost every friend.

There are men who deeply sympathize with these views of justification ; men who are waked to thought; men who predict a large influence, even for humble means, to preaching in a consistent way justification by works (Rom. ii: 13). There might be a growing horror kindled, and a broken-hearted surprise, that we, who have been most bitter against the Pope, and most bewildered by the possibilities of a reviving ritualism, should find the monster in ourselves; and that we have made the very simplicities of faith a soul-destroying and church-corrupting instrument of superstition.

But publish this book, it will be said, and one man at least may leave the enterprise.

Nay, all that he has ever writ, and all that he may hope to write, will be a voice against it.

The advocate of a bare belief, who has cut off from it all elements of holiness, will take courage in the very fact, that the impulse to oppose him is so soon caught by other gusts, and is so soon showing its source by quarreling with other doctrines of evangelical Christianity.

What am I to do therefore? It would be such a pleasure to remain in shelter! Why not take one thing at a time? If Justification be the more important point, why not prefer that, and have something posthumous for the other?

This has been said to me.

But, unfortunately, we are all confessors. Each lives not a day but he avows the confession of his faith. There are honesties in this matter. And, though I might remain concealed, and not renew my avowals but upon some change of place; yet what for a defence is that? Do I not virtually avow, every day and hour, my original confession?

I will not meet my brethren, therefore, with anything concealed.

But, now; a little on the other side.

When I finished my "Metaphysics," and found that I differed from the reigning school; and when, under the light of an ethical belief, I criticised ten points in our prevalent dogmatic forms; * and when, at a later date, I conceived the two monographs that will perhaps be bound up with this,—I began to take the alarm. My "Metaphysics" might be a matter of free lance. My "Fetich" had been confessed as true by a majority of Calvinistic chairs.† These monographs could not be mortally astray. But where was this thing to end? I might, thus far, not be amenable to my church; but where further? I began to be anxious about the working of my mind. And, as a man must follow it wherever it will lead, I began to look eagerly ahead, and ask, where an erring intellect would carry me next, against the opinions of bodies of my brethren.

I did the only thing practicable. I plunged into my whole theology. Having returned from a lengthened route, made necessary by philosophical publication, I did what the old man does who taps the wheels after they come from a trip. I wished to see if I was sound. And, therefore, with as much prayer as I could offer, and with abundant purpose to be true, I studied the whole system of our faith; and came out, as I was grateful to find, thoroughly and emphatically fixed on every point of our common soteriology.

So eminent was this, that I found myself utterly

---

* See "*Fetich in Theology.*" † In America.

opposed to the usual changes that have been proposed for our Confession. Depravity; I found it philosophical. I found it of every faculty, and in every act. Why not call it "total"? I found there were but two commandments, and I kept neither; and, therefore, I had nothing to propose in the way of limit or qualification. Imputation; I found it forensic. Adam; I found him my ruin. He corrupted me naturally; but he corrupted me, also, punitively. That is, a bad child cannot come from a father as an acorn does from an oak; but there must be justice in it. There must be some arrangement of law, to justify my corruption by my parents. Redemption; I believed it penal; conversion, immediate; regeneration, gracious; our call, effectual; our helplessness, entire; and our atonement, adoption and sanctification all that they are ever made, and more, than by these mere trust believers. Moreover, I believed in Christ. I found him to be literally God: not God in the sense that he was not a man, or in a way that none of us entertain it, viz., that the true man was directly, and *qua* man, transmutedly the Almighty; but that he was God-man, having God incarnate in him : and that he was all, and more than all, that the most who have been the purest in the church have glorified as the actual Almighty.

Moreover, I ennobled his redemption. Had he been a man, I could not trust him : or an angel ; or a God in the Arian sense; or divine after the Socinian pattern. To me, he was the Maker of the universe ; and more God in the actual sense, than he could be, under my old ideas.

Thus there emerged out of all my inquisition a remarkably rigid faith; and when I added that I was a *jure divino* churchman; and a far firmer believer of Scriptural Presbytery than the great majority of my brethren: and when I rechallenged all this, and found it seated in my thought, and impossible to be removed in any usual intellectual possibility at my time of life, I felt quieted from restless fever, and riveted in devoted affection to the communion in which I had been brought up.

Alas for me! that I should have any fear that I must be detruded out of it!

In the midst of all these studies, I found one great central object disappearing out of the firmament of my confession. It has been a singular history. Years ago I had a similar onsault. In reading the word of God, the Trinity suddenly deserted me. I said, It has been a fanciful conceit. I said, The divinity of kings, the right to persecute, the blood of Abraham, the grace of baptism, the sacrifice of the mass, have reigned unchallenged in the church. They are the "unsanctioned fables" of which Paul speaks (1 Tim. iv: 7). Now are we clear of such like? I was clear that we were not. And there broke upon me with dismay the panic-driven discovery that there was no Trinity; that it was all a figment; that it was, not odious to reason, but absent from the Word; and I searched and searched and searched, and the discovery almost was, that the Bible was colorless of such a dogma, and, by any reasonable mode, could not be made to teach those hypostatic differences.

But I rallied. I thought of this text; "The

glory that I had with thee" (Jo. xvii: 5); I thought of this, " Thou Lord in the beginning" (Heb. i: 10); I thought of this, " By whom were all things created" (Col. i: 16); I thought of this, " Of the Father, and of the Son, and of the Holy Ghost" (Matt. xxviii: 19): I made a thorough reinspection of the proofs, and found myself restored to my old impressions.

I had almost forgotten it.

But now, a second time, at the same weak places, when I was inviting a thorough review, there came upon me the same assault; and the texts that had stood by the doctrine, utterly failed me.

Stirred, as I naturally would be, where my very church was slipping away from me, I awoke to the full seriousness of the case. I gave up everything. For three months I did nothing but inspect the Trinity. A library happened to be near, uncommonly rich in all that literature, and I did the best I could. I scouted very soon all the criticisms of *reason*, except perhaps those that doubted whether there was any thought under the word " Person." I saw it was not a Bible word. But my investigations of *Scripture* led me to a verdict like this,—that if the Bible taught the Trinity, it taught the Mass more and better; that its teaching both was fancied by a mistake of figures; that its teaching either was one of the vagaries of the human heart; and that its teaching neither would long ago have been the faith, if the hypostatic distinctions of the Almighty disturbed our ransom in the same serious way as did the dishonored sacrament.

This, then, was the process of the study. Now

for the result. I do not believe in the Trinity. It may be said, You are a Sabellian. You believe that the Father is God, and the Son is God, and the Spirit is God. But you do not believe in the hypostatic difference that subsists between them. You believe in a modality. You believe that the Creator is God, and the Redeemer is God, and the Sanctifier is God; and that these are but modal differences that make up the triplicity of the Almighty.

I would have no objection to that. That is, I hold that these names are all different, for that these offices all exist. These divine appellatives have each a different sense. I would have no objection to the man who made these senses the divisions of a sermon; for undoubtedly God has all these features of versatile administration. But I will not so take that critical number, THREE, as to suppose that there is a norm in it; and that the infinite modalities of God are circumscribed by any Trinity. I will not admit any intended threeness. And after my three months' wrestle, I will speak in this way,—"They call him Indra, Mitra, Varuna, Agni; then he is the beautiful-winged heavenly Garutmat: that which is One, the wise call it in divers manners: they call it Agni, Yama, Mâterisvan" (*Rig-veda* I. 164, 46): "Wise poets make the beautiful-winged, though he is one, manifold by words" (*R–v.* x: 114, 5).

Now, to be a great deal more precise. All that Dr. Alexander and Francis Turretin would impute of Deity to Christ, I do, and perhaps more. That is I put the whole Godhead in him. I make the Father, as he himself seems to do (Jo. v: 19, 26, 36;

vi : 57 ; x : 29, 30, 36), his Godhead. My gospel, therefore, is safe : my redemption, perfect. Jehovah, among the old Jews, was Christ moving about without his incarnation ; and, if you ask me what that means, I would say, It was God, under whatever name, administering in the name of Emmanuel : pardoning on the base of his obedience ; creating on the faith of his advent; and intending, in the fullness of time, to unite himself with him as one person, and to be, as plenary God, what we have imagined as being the Eternally Begotten.

The difficulties of this will hereafter be relieved by Scripture.

I wish only to say, that God eternally, and before his Incarnation, is, to me, One Person ; that God eternally, after his incarnation, is, as God, One Person ; that, Spirit, Word, and Jehovah, he is but describing himself as the glorious Almighty ; and that, when I pray for the Spirit ; or reverence the Son ; or worship the Father,—I am thinking of the One Personal God : and that it would have been infinitely better never to load the faith with the Platonic Trinity.

You may say, Explain all that.

And I do it eagerly.

"That the doctrine of the Trinity was indebted for its development to Christology, is universally acknowledged" (Dorner, I. A. p. 354). Undoubtedly the shock that this preface occasions, is due to our thought for the gospel. But suppose the gospel is in no sense implicated. Suppose the Arian affects our faith, and destroys our ransom ; and suppose the

Socinian is just as dangerous. Suppose the Deity of Christ, and the helplessness of sin, and the preciousness of ransom, have all been denied, by previous impugners of the Trinity, till they have swollen themselves into monsters of unbelief. May not that now be just the difficulty? And suppose it all at last different. Suppose a new dissection. Suppose the gospel gloriously honored. Suppose the scheme carved deeper; and the strength of God's magisterial claim actually heightened. Suppose redemption made to stand apart like the works of a watch, and the metaphysics of the Deity separate like the case that holds them in; should anti-trinity thought be, any more, looked upon as fatal? And would it not be a preposterous stand; if I trust in Christ; and lean upon him as God: if I take his blood, and wash myself in it as the divine redemption: if I make him the whole Jehovah, and think he will reign so forever and forever: if I pray for his Spirit, but only think that "the Lord is that Spirit" (2 Cor. iii: 17), and that in praying for the Spirit I am praying for God,—to impugn me like mortal heretics?—praying for Christ, or praying for the Father, or, if you please, praying for grace in any guise in which it may be revealed most beautifully, to say, that, because I doubt a hypostatic difference, therefore, in what men are not sure they have an idea at all, I wreck my faith, and must be cast out of my communion.

And that brings me to the last point.

I have determined to be scrupulously exact with my brethren. I desire to be humble, too, and modest as to the belief that I am right. How unspeakably absurd the attitude of one just in my place to arrogate the discovery of the light, when the very monarchs of the world's thought have been piously and earnestly against him!

But I must do something.

I had thought of an immediate interview with my Presbytery. But my friends entreat that I will test every position to the very last; and that if I find myself irreclaimably fixed, the result of all this industry and care may be, to offer my beliefs in the way most easily to be inspected by those above me.

That, then, is my plan.

But what will be the result? Would to God I exactly knew.

I am clear thus far. I had better not resign my position in the church. I doubt the legality of such a move. But if it were legal, why should I do it? I could but swim back thitherward as soon as I was able. Why should I not invite my Presbytery to keep me in?

And, now, as to the possibility of that.

Two things occur to me.

(1) In the first place, there are differences already. Turretin believes that Christ was generated by the Father. So does our Confession. A member of my Presbytery teaches that that is no where taught in Scripture. Our creed teaches a marked Eschatology, conspicuous in which is the advent of Christ, and a judgment at the last day. A member of my Presbytery teaches a premillenarian scheme; and traverses much in my Confession. So of an external church. My Confession accentuates it. My brethren make

light of it. The six days' creation : that is taught in our symbols. Who believes it? I myself would be, perhaps, one of the few men in my Presbytery to adhere prevailingly to the ancient thinking. Now, who will draw the line? A man publishes one year a *kenosis* of the Deity, and an actual suffering of God on the cross on Calvary. He is an excellent brother, and he is made the Moderator of the next Assembly. Undoubtedly, then, difference from the Confession will not cast a man out of the Church. The question is, How serious is it? And my course seems to be to defend my belief. If I can make it appear secondary; if I can show that I hold the vitals of the gospel; if I can prove that I am not a Socinian; if I can show that I approach my faith from another quarter; if I can show that Arminius and Pelagius and Arius have neither tampered with me; but that I am a high Calvinist in all the realities of my creed, —then my Presbytery will have to determine whether one symptom of a Socinian's belief cannot become a feature in a far lesser disease, and whether a hypostatic difference in the Godhead is in such sense vital to the faith, that a minister must go out of his church, even if he puts the WHOLE GODHEAD in Christ, and builds on that scheme a perfect redemption.

The Presbytery must decide.

(2) But may I not say another thing; How is a great church like ours to be corrected of any error? It may be answered, It has none. But is that certain? The time was when this very church persecuted. The time was when it was largely Jacobite. Across the sea it is still Erastian. In some cases at

least, it holds sacramental error. What is the relief? Must it be groomed with a foreign comb; or may it do something to its own recuperation?

Suppose the Trinity were a mistake; suppose it had bestrid the gospel in its earlier planting. Suppose it were a Platonic set, grafted by the Jews, and inarched from them into the faith of Christians. Suppose that John opposed it, and that his first strong text was meant to fence it out (Jo. i: 1),—how is the church to become satisfied of that? Why may there not be a little pause? And why must it be by bell and torch that the church must expel the truth, and that the light must go out from established fanes, and shine into some shieling church, that must become, in turn, the inveterate oppressor?

May God in his infinite mercy protect the truth! And if there be any who pity me, may they offer this prayer,—first, that I may be brought out of dangerous mistake; and, second, that I may behave humbly and well; so that when I have gained time enough to have my brethren thoroughly look into my case to see whether I am in dangerous error, or to see whether they themselves are certain of their faith, I may, if the Church is against me, do nothing to distract her; but step aside, with a modest doubt of myself, and with a heightened earnestness, to pray and find out, after such a verdict, what can really be known of the truth of the Almighty.

JNO. MILLER.

PRINCETON, Oct. 2d, 1876.

CONTENTS.

I.

THE TRINITY AND REASON.......................... 23

CHAPTER I.

THE TRINITY NOT TO BE JUDGED BY REASON............... 23

CHAPTER II.

THE TRINITY TO GIVE SOME IDEA OF ITSELF TO REASON .. 26

CHAPTER III.

THE TRINITY WITH NO IDEA: NO IDEA, EVER ATTEMPTED FOR A TRINITY, NOT PRONOUNCED NO IDEA AT ALL BY ACCEPTED TRINITARIANS............................ 27

CHAPTER IV.

THE TRINITY WITH NO SHELTER IN INFALLIBILITY.......... 30

CHAPTER V.

THE TRINITY ACCOUNTED FOR BY HISTORY................ 33

II.

	PAGE
THE TRINITY AND SCRIPTURE	39

CHAPTER I.

METHOD OF TREATMENT	39

CHAPTER II.

GOD THE HOLY GHOST	41
§ 1. The Unity of God	41
§ 2. The Unity of God's Person not Disturbed by Different Names	43
§ 3. The Unity of God's Person not Disturbed by Emblems	44
§ 4. The Unity of God's Person not Disturbed by His Holy Spirit	45
§ 5. The Unity of God's Person not to be Disturbed by Grammatic Differences—and first, not by Differences of Person	48
§ 6. The Unity of God's Person not Disturbed by Differences of Gender	50
§ 7. The Unity of God's Person not Disturbed by Difference of Number	54
§ 8. The Unity of God's Person not Disturbed by Difference of Case	56
§ 9. The Unity of God's Person not Disturbed by any other Differences	58
§ 10. No Distinct Personality of the Spirit	67

CHAPTER III.

GOD THE SON	72
§ 1. The Deity of the Son	72
§ 2. The Humanity of the Son	72
§ 3. The Begetting of the Son	73

	PAGE
§ 4. *The Son and the Spirit*	76
§ 5. *The Son and the Father*	78
§ 6. *The Son as Jehovah*	80
§ 7. *The Son as Sent*	81
§ 8. *The Son as Wisdom*	82
§ 9. *The Son and the Logos*	83
§10. *The Son and the Creation*	90
§11. *The Son's Pre-existence*	100
§12. *Angel of Jehovah*	109
§13. *The Son as Father, Son and Holy Ghost*	112

CHAPTER IV.

GOD THE FATHER 112

§ 1. *Meaning of the Name*	112
§ 2. *No Name or Work Sacred to One Person*	115
§ 3. *The Father as Son*	117
§ 4. *The Father as Spirit*	119
§ 5. *The Father as Jehovah*	121
§ 6. *The Father and His Glory*	125
§ 7. *The Baptismal Formula*	127
§ 8. *The Apostolic Benediction*	130
§ 9. *The Scene at Jordan*	131

CHAPTER V.

THE TRINITY NOTHING TO THE GOSPEL 132

§ 1. *What are the Gospel Ideas?*	132
§ 2. *The Incarnation*	134
§ 3. *Redemption*	134
§ 4. *Mediation*	134
§ 5. *Intercession*	137
§ 6. *Regeneration*	141
§ 7. *Justification*	142
§ 8. *Adoption*	144
§ 9. *Judgment*	145
§10. *Sanctification*	145
§11. *Glorification*	146

III.

CONCLUSION... 148

CHAPTER I.

THE SCANDAL OF THIS BOOK 148

CHAPTER II.

THE BENEFIT OF THIS BOOK............................ 151

I.

THE TRINITY AND REASON.

CHAPTER I.

The Trinity not to be Judged by Reason.

I WISH to set forward the statement, that I am moved to this book by Scripture. In order to do this, I hold the ground that the Trinity is not to be judged by reason. In order to do this, I follow that statement, and show that it is very peculiar. *Everything* is to be judged by reason. Until it be true that the eye is no judge of color, it will never be true that reason is no judge of anything; for, in fact, there is no judge of anything but reason; and of all that our race can conceive, reason is the sole and universal arbiter.

What is meant, therefore, by reason being no judge of the Trinity? Let me explain by the instance of gravitation. Reaching far back to absolute sight, and to those most obstinate of all demonstrators of truth, mathematical figures, the mind has been forced into the faith that there is a gravitation. It is no judge of the phenomena, afterward. The man who is prolific of difficulties, and tells us that gravitation is impossible; and who backs up his thought by saying that the sun is ninety-four millions of miles away, and that its grappling the earth over that distance is a sheer conceit, we laugh at. Let the sun get over his own difficulties. We have forever demonstrated the truth, that he does attract; and all inter-situated puzzles we neglect. Reason is a judge of everything; but, having made her judgment back at the original truth, we know what we mean by saying, that she is no judge of the doctrine afterward.

So of the Trinity. In a way that is universal and confessed, reason has made her judgment of the word of God. This is a broad field; and she has examined it thoroughly. This is the all-comprehensive fact; and she has established it by outward and inward evidence. She has come to the strongest faith (and no disciple of the Redeemer will lightly cavil at it), that the Bible is the voice of the Almighty; and this, not by mystic partialities, but by reasonable tests, which lift her ever afterward above the fear of what is contained in the recognized canon.

This is what is meant by reason being no judge of the Trinity.

The Papist has a kindred submissiveness. He does not deny the authority of reason; but he has spent all her power in examining into the authority of the Church. There has been his original question. He holds you to be right in testing him there. And, if you would witness patience, you have but to look at his books on the church. Where you are building up the authority of Scripture, he is laying the corner stone of Zion; and it is only after you have accepted the church, that he lays his hand upon your mouth, and tells you that you have no right of private judgment afterward.

And to show how sincere we are in all this, we say plainly, If the Mass were in the Bible, we would believe the Mass. The Papist believes it on the authority of the Church. We would believe it on the authority of Scripture. And, in either case, man's appeal is to his rational nature; for, in the one case, it has led him to accept the Church, and in the other, Scripture; and it is only on the lower ground, that he denies, in such things as the Trinity and the Mass, any right to the judgments of the mind.

But it may be said, What if a doctrine seems flat against reason? Even then I would not disown it. We have seen the reasonableness of this in the instance of gravitation. If Paul tells me to persecute the heretic, I will do so, as the voice of the Almighty; if he pronounces boldly upon the truth of Jacobitism, I am a Jacobite; if he tells me that Christ is in the wafer, I believe it: and my principle is here:—I am under a great hardship, and my conscience revolts at the texts, but I am the devotee of a great process. I have gone through all labored proofs. My conscience, and everything besides, pronounces for the Bible; and, when that great huge fact comes athwart that lesser one, a belief in transubstantiation, I yield. Bring me any miserable faith that does not positively deny the grace of the Almighty, and, if you can deceive me so far as to make it Scriptural, I will accept it; and on the sheer base that I have accepted the word of God as "the only infallible rule of faith and practice."

CHAPTER II.

The Trinity to Give some Idea of itself to Reason.

BUT, though we admit that the Trinity is not to be judged by reason; and though the fact of transubstantiation, if you will prove that it is taught in the word of God, I will compound for as made possible by some mysterious miracle; though I will become an Inquisitor, in spite of all its contradiction of conscience, and will get over this difficulty by remembering that heretics are the property of God; though I will believe in the right of kings, to the extent of enduring a bad king even though I could unseat him, if you will convince me that God ordains it; and I will hold He is the Lord of Providence, and can adjust the consequences of all His commands,—yet there is one right that reason retains, and that is, to know distinctly what it is that it believes. To say, I believe in the Mass, and to be left with nothing but the four letters; or to say, I am a Jacobite, or, if you please, I am an Inquisitor, and leave me no idea under the formula professed,—is of course the most awful solecism. And, therefore, coming now to the case of the Trinity, if when you come to propound the doctrine, you give me positively no conception of it, it is preposterous beyond the need of a discussion. I wish to draw a distinction between understanding a doctrine, and having a conception of it. I understand no doctrine under the sun. I have a conception of every doctrine. That is to say, No doctrine can possibly be embraced, that remains wrapt up in an expression, so that positively no thought comes out from what is spoken. I wish to insist upon this, upon the very outset of our teaching. What is the Trinity? It may be said, It is the doctrine of the Three in One. Of course our first landing place is upon the reserve that God is Three in a different sense from his being One. But when we come to remember, this is a mere speech, this is a mere exsiccated shell; this is no form of thought, till we say what the sense is. And there, now, precisely is our position. Reason is no judge of that sense after it is once announced. But the Trinity is no doctrine at all, and, therefore, in the court of intellect must be held by hypocrites; or else some conception must be given, in what sense God can be Three, and yet the most simple of all possible existence.

Think of excommunicating a man from the Church for failing to believe that of which you can give him no idea!

CHAPTER III.

THE TRINITY WITH NO IDEA: NO IDEA, EVER ATTEMPTED FOR A TRINITY, NOT PRONOUNCED NO IDEA AT ALL BY ACCEPTED TRINITARIANS.

AND I am the more confirmed in this careful preliminary, because every idea of Trinitarianism that has ever been held, has been declared to be no idea at all by accepted Trinitarians. I confess that this is no positive argument. In the first place, it is

impossible to declare who are accepted Trinitarians
In the second place, the argument would not be
positive, if we could. There might be ten men that
held a particular doctrine; and each nine might denounce the tenth, in turn, as holding it in a form
that is perfectly unmeaning. This would not
amount to refutation. All the classes of nine might
be wrong, and yet, if one reflects a moment, one
man of the ten might survive as right.

Let me illustrate. (1) Our Confession speaks of
the " Eternally Begotten." The idea there contained
is, that the Second Person of the Trinity is eternally
derived. Hosts of thinkers pronounce that unmeaning. And one of our most distinguished divines disagrees with Turrettin; would conceive derivation
unthinkable; and boldly declares that it is not
taught in the word of God (Hodge, Theol. V. i : p.
486). It will be noticed, therefore, that a man who
denies the Trinity altogether, is but denying that
which, in one form or other, has been denounced as
senseless by the most pious of the orthodox.

Again :—

(2) The Trinity has been held to be the One
conscious Divinity. Sherlock objected to this; and
denied, in that case, the possibility of threeness. He
found in the Bible separate wills; and proclaimed, as
his notion of all that could be thought of as Three,
separate consciousnesses. John Howe partially defended him. The Church broke out against him.
And, yet, he never lost his See: and, though his
belief was unvarnished Polytheism, yet it was distinctly enforced, on the principle we mentioned,—

that the opposite was unmeaning; that a belief requires something to be conceived; and that, if God is Three Persons, it is like saying he is a gnoot, or Abracadabra, unless it is a tri-personal Three, in the sense of separate intelligence.

(3) Andover has furnished another theory. Schleiermacher, explaining Sabellius, has rather adopted his thought, that the Trinity became a Trinity in time: that God did not eternally create; and that he did not eternally redeem: that, therefore, he became each of these in time: that the Trinity is the Creator and Redeemer and Sanctifier; and that, therefore, God grew to be these; and that this is the meaning of the inspired Trinity.

Moses Stuart modified this into a scheme. He said; and this was the foundation of his system; that what God lived to become in time, he was fitted to become from all eternity. And, therefore, his fitness to become this or that, was his trine relation. Accordingly, without pursuing this account, it will still farther illustrate our understood position. This learned man's appeal was to the *uselessness of the unmeaning;* and, seeming to forget that God was fit for a multiplicity of things from all eternity; that he came to paint black, and to paint yellow; that he came to make stars, and to make flowers; and that it was impossible to distinguish between what might be called Trinitarian fitnesses, and fitnesses for less hypostatic things,—he nevertheless continued in the church, unchallenged; and yet managed to add another whole theory to the faith, which lived only by denouncing everything else as vague and notionless.

CHAPTER IV.

THE TRINITY WITH NO SHELTER IN INFALLIBILITY.

THUS the doctrine is like Maelzell's Chess-Player. We open each door in turn, and there is nothing in it. Yes, some one will say, there was a man in the Chess-Player, after all. I grant it; but on terms that no avowed Trinitarian will be willing to admit. There was a man in the Chess-Player, because, before each opening, he altered his position. A man proposes a Trinity: another man exposes it. He offers his in turn, and some third man shows there is nothing in it. He asseverates another, and a fourth man opens that door, and finds it empty. Now, a notion can be supported in this way; but it is, as a missile is, by flying through the air. I do not make a point of all this; and I discard reason as an intermediary. But this I do say, that reason ought not to be suborned *against* us.

Try any company.

Go among twenty ministers, and say,—Our fellow presbyter has denied the doctrine of the Trinity. The very first bubbling up of censure will be from that form of reason which is embalmed in the vote of the vast body of believers. The arrogance of the presbyter!—is the first thing that will strike every body. But how long should this outcry last? Always, if the Church is infallible; and, past doubt, the Church *is* infallible in vital matters. Let us consider this. There has always been a church. There cannot be a church without a gospel. There cannot be a gospel if there be damning error. Immunity from damning error is of the very faith of the gospel. And, therefore, when Papists claim infallibility, they are groping after some truth. And he is not hastily advised, who, convinced of the piety of his Zion, claims that Christ keeps it (Matt. xvi: 18; xxviii: 20), and holds that, let the Trinity be among the vitals of the scheme of grace, it is among the infallibilities of true believers.

But now, definitely, there is covered up the very question.

The ritualist holds that baptism is of necessity to grace. If so, it is vital. And if so, some church will possess it.

The orthodox hold, that Christ is necessary to pardon. If so, that is vital. And if so, the church will never lose that doctrine.

It is this true figure of infallibility that moves darkly in the background, and gives rancor to religious hate; for when a man has been sufficiently ridiculed for pitting himself against the profound and pious, then this that is ghostly comes in, and he is made to tremble for his pride in arraying himself against the church of the Redeemer.

How, then, may we meet infallibility? By rejoicing and trusting in it; and by singing psalms to God that we are invulnerable through our infallible Redeemer: but not in any way that is prescriptive. Paul gives the rule:—" Prove all things. Hold fast that which is good." Doctrine must be vital first; infallible afterward. Otherwise Luther was apostate.

Here is a fellow presbyter. He comes to us in the fairest way. He invites us to the closest scrutiny. He says, Here is my system of Christ. I believe that the Trinity, like the Old Man of the Sea, has jumped npon the back of Sinbad, and made Christianity coarse and heavy through all its journey. I believe it is a robbery of the heathen. I believe it awakened Mohammed. I believe it has worn out missionaries. I believe it has kept back Pagans, who were obliged to perish in their sins, while their nation waited to learn an "unsanctioned fable" (1 Tim. iv: 7). I believe the great God in heaven was born himself into Jesus, "and so was and continueth to be, God and man, in two distinct natures, and one person, forever" (Sh. Catechism, Qu. 21). I believe just this is sufficient; and that ransom, and grace, and divine power, and all that was needed of sacrifice, and that all that there will ever be of glory, is sufficiently secured in this One Person, Jehovah.

And if a Christian says to me, Avaunt as a heretic, and never examines my faith, and never says, Is this discriminateness sufficient? if he never says, Is not the Trinity with this man a minor doctrine? and, even if he be in error, does he not hold the chief truths? and has he not a well knit system; and does he not seem to say all for Christ except that there is a hypostatic difference between him and the Father —if he has never done any thing for me like that, I'll tell you what he is like; he is like the man that threw the first stone at Stephen, because he proclaimed the Galilean; he is like the court that imprisoned Ken because he refused the Declaration; he is like the priests that burned Huss on the plea that he decried the sacrament. And there is a family likeness which I wish particularly to press; which claims a just infallibility, but which sins only in this, —that it brings within the reach of that blessing of God minor things, under the claim that these are of the essentials of salvation.

Men are not to choose how able shall be the man who discovers error. The mouse is not to be weighed who eats the lion out of the net. Galileans bearded Jewry. A miner's son shook St. Peter's. Poor peasant women sickened the world of martyrdoms. And if the humblest minister can put the Trinity alongside of the consecrated wafer, and make both seem figments of the sense, the Church has nothing to do but to examine it, and, laying all prerogative apart, give thanks for her infallible life, when she has thoroughly understood and thoroughly made good that it is fatal.*

CHAPTER V.

The Trinity Accounted for by History.

Any of us would say, before study, that the Trinity is revealed in the Old Testament. Any of us would at least declare, that it was revealed in the

---

* Is there not something that proves the Trinity a superstition in the very Creed of Athanasius, and in the fact that the church has not awoke her thunders against that long ago. Let us quote a part of it. "Whosoever will be saved must hold the Catholic faith. The Catholic faith is this,—that we worship one God in Trinity, and Trinity in Unity, neither confounding the persons nor dividing the substance. For there are three persons, but one Godhead. The Father is neither

Bible. Any of us would suppose, that it was taught in the first age of the church.

Now, to cut off all wandering, and to confine ourselves to the testimony of Scripture, I would say that all these things have been doubted, and doubted too by Trinitarians themselves. Athanasius holds that the Jews knew nothing of a Trinity. I mention other names in the margin.* Bellarmin holds that it is no where taught in Scripture. He builds it on tradition. Petavius holds that it was not caught by tradition. That is, he quotes from the fathers, and shows that it was not known in the first age of the

---

made, created, nor begotten. The Son is of the Father alone, not made, nor created, but begotten. The Holy Ghost is of the Father and the Son, neither made, nor created, nor begotten, but proceeding; and in this Trinity none is afore or after another; none is greater or less than another. This is the Catholic faith, WHICH EXCEPT A MAN BELIEVE FAITHFULLY, HE CANNOT BE SAVED." That this spurious creed, fraudulently palmed upon the church, and which, whatever Athanasius might have thought of it, never saw Athanasius, and was written centuries after he was dead,—should survive with vigor, and be treated with general respect, is itself an invitation, I think, to a reinvestigation of the whole subject; and to a strong suspicion of a faith that speaks so definitely of inconceivable things; and wields so insolently the anathemas of heaven for that of which the good people of an earlier world must certainly have had no idea.

* " The Papists deny that the doctrine of the Trinity is to be found in Scripture. See this plainly taught and urged by Card. Hosius, *de Auth. S. Scrip.* L. III: p. 33: Gordonius Hunlaeus, *Cont. Tim. Comb. de Verbo Dei,* c. 19; Gretserus and Zanerus, *in Colloquio Ratisbon;* Vega, Possevin, Wickius. . . These learned men, especially Bellarmin, and Wickius after him, have urged all the Scriptures they could, with the utmost industry, find out in this cause, and yet, after all, they acknowledge their insufficiency and obscurity."—*Locke's Commonplace Book. King's Life of Locke,* Vol. II. p. 104.

church.* Now what does that prove? Why, that tradition is very colorless; and that reason can do very little, on that tack, to relieve the faith.

Now, another matter.

History accounts for things.

If I am waked up by Scripture, and utter a cry, Why, where is the Trinity? and suddenly search, and find myself deserted of the idea, I naturally ask, How did it arise? and not in a way that we can pronounce decisive, and yet in quite a sufficient way, we find how it could have arisen.

Plato invented a Trinity: some think, by himself; some think, out of a spark of tradition. It is not in a form that Christians love; and many deny that it had any common origin with ours. While Plato was working in the schools, Rabbis were working in the Law, and making changes in it; that is, they were writing Targums, that is to say, paraphrases of the text. These were read in the Synagogues. One of the changes that the paraphrases made was, to put " Word of Jehovah" for " Jehovah." They found it once or twice (Ps. xxxiii: 6; cv: 19), and it fell in with reigning thought, and they took out the word " Jehovah," and they put in " Word of Jehovah" two hundred times. The Jewish ear, accordingly, was accustomed to it; and, when Alexandria was built, and the Septuagint was written, and the Alexandria Jews became the repositories of law, Philo and the men that preceded him worked upon these Targums, and brought in Platonic aid; and the writings remain which actually cast the Scrip-

* *Pet. de Trin.* I. 5, 7 : 8, 2.

tures into Platonic moulds. Now, what was the result? Confessedly a species of Arianism. These men deified the Word: not as I do, by making it a name of God; but contrariwise, by making it an emanation. They did not all agree: and Philo himself was better than others of the school; but the tendency was this,—to say, The Word was an emanation. It was not God: and it was not man; but it was between them. It was not God; and it was not a creature; but it was an emanation. It was not eternal; and it was not yet to arise; but it was intermediate and in time. The distinct teaching was, that the Word was an emanation from God; subordinate; intermediate; and the origin of all the creatures.

Thence bring it to account that this teaching was in all the schools; and that John came upon the stage when pious thought was helplessly saturated with all these ideas.

What was he to do with them? Reply? Why, they were chameleon-like; and had no fixed expression. Not reply? Why, that would be to be waterlogged with hopeless prevarications. What could he do? Precisely what he did do. "In the beginning was the Word;" thus shearing away all thought of an emanation in time: "And the Word was with God" (E. V). Let me alter that at once. The preposition never means *with*.* We have the

---

* Perhaps I had better temper this by saying, that the few exceptions that might be imagined (as Mar. vi: 3; Matt. xiii: 56), are not absolute exceptions; and perhaps I had better refer, for the facts about this preposition, to Gesenius. He is a fair party to quote, be-

expression, " things pertaining to God" (E. V.: Heb. ii : 17; v: 1). The preposition means "*towards*," or "*pertaining to.*" Let us read it so. " In the beginning was the Word, and the Word pertained to God." That is, it did not emanate and go out and become subordinate and intermediate, but it was simply God's word. It was like God's arm, or God's power. It was just God expressing himself, and God revealing himself, as though he had said, like Paul, " Whom therefore ye ignorantly worship, him declare I unto you" (Acts xvii: 23).

But, to cut off all mistake, he gives another and most trenchant expression. " In the beginning was the Word, and the Word pertained to God, and God was the Word." Alford admits that, if it be translated this way, it denies the Trinity! and old Middleton has, for decades, stood like a tower, to say that the Greek must be reversed. It is a judgment upon the Greek article (Gram. iii. s. 4, § 1); but the finest scholars have now reversed that opinion (Winer, Glassius, *etc.*). The old Vulgate never obeyed it. And the article has another way to account for itself, viz., that it is the specific mark that it is " *the*" Word in the great reigning sense,—which, John would teach, was nothing but the Almighty.

But we are anticipating. We are not among Scriptures yet. We quote this in the way of historic elucidation.

We verily believe much could be made of his-

cause his very principles are, to the very utmost bent, to supply the force of " *with*" in this very passage. And yet the strict reader will see, for all that, which way his authority inclines. See, also, Winer.

tory; and that we could trace the Trinity like the fossils in a rock. Indeed, we think that it is impossible that it was an apostolic dogma, if for no other reason than that it is thought vital, and that it is laid down so infinitely not so in their books. But let all this pass. We are now finishing our account of reason; and all we wish to do is, to bind it hand and foot, now that we have got out of it a decision for the canon, while we ask, simply, what that canon says. Let us *suppose* an idea. Let us *imagine* that we apprehend it. Let it be, with more or less sense, *triplicity in unity;* and while with reverent appeal we beg to be enlightened in the word, let reason, on the other side, not treat us in any way we do not deserve, after our appeal, like Paul's, has gone to a higher tribunal.

II.

THE TRINITY AND SCRIPTURE.

CHAPTER I.

Method of Treatment.

The best way to prove a doctrine is to state it clearly, and then show, text by text, that it is supported in the word of God. This is the method of expert scientists, when they discard a theory like emission, and establish a doctrine like undulation, as the true theory of light. It is eminently the natural way. They state their theory clearly, and, then, open the book of nature; and their highest exultation is, when fact after fact weaves beautifully in, and when such a phenomenon as two light rays fitting wave into wave and producing darkness, demonstrates the undulation of the ether, rather than its direct emission.

Should I take this most natural plan, therefore, I should, first, state my express doctrine of God. I should say, God is one person. I should say, God is incarnate in Christ. I should say, No hypostatic difference separates off the Father from the Son; but the one God is Emmanuel. God with us. I would say, God furnishes a Mediator, the Man Christ Jesus; and the suitedness of that Mediator is, first, that he is a man, to stand between God and us, and, second, that he is God, to bring the whole being of the Godhead in to give value to his atonement, and to furnish the regenerating power; the idea being that, on the side of God, the Father and the Son are one; and that it is only on the side of man that the Son stands off from the Father, and can be looked upon, with the higher truth in the emblem, as a glorious Mediator (1 Tim. ii: 5).

Then my part would be, to trace this in the Word: to show, wherever I read, that my doctrine is the one advanced, and not the doctrine of the Trinity; to show that one agrees, and the other does not agree, with the main tenor of the book; and to show, as I confidently might, that where the Trinitarian has spun a tenuous thread of apparent connection for his scheme, the Bible itself breaks it; that is, that a discrepance in God, shadowily made out by a discrepance in facts or titles, is carefully obliterated; some wave of simple denial coming up from the Word, to wash out the lines of distinction that might seem to have been implied in other passages.

This plan we should have preferred. This plan would be noble, for example, in blotting out from the dream of the church baptismal regeneration.

But now, simply to meet a prejudice, I take another. Theology is an intricate scheme; and men have gotten to believe that anything can be tortured out of the Bible. If I state my theory, and then go on to find it, men will say, and say truly, that my glow of enthusiasm is just that which infidels have, when they are picking up the ingots of truth, as they regard them, in physical nature.

My plan, therefore, will be worse, but more conciliating. I will not take theism bereft of hypostases, and then prove it; but I will take my adversary's ground, and follow it along as long as it will bear me; and when I come to the spot where Scripture forsakes it, I will put the staff into my neighbor's hands. I will not frame a doctrine, and then support it; for the mass will say, I am expounding to suit myself. But I am going to take my neighbor's doctrine, and follow it along as far as we agree. And where we differ, I am going to make my neighbor expound. In other words, I am going to take the doctrine of the Trinity, and strip it of all in which we all agree; and then I am going to take the dry husk that remains, bereft of all that I can see established, and ask my neighbor to establish it; in other words take the HYPOSTATIC DIFFERENCES, which are the only points which this book rejects, and simply stand on my watch, and refuse anything baseless that may be supposed to cover them.

CHAPTER II.

GOD THE HOLY GHOST.

§ 1. *The Unity of God.*

ACTING on this method,—My neighbor and I agree in the unity of Jehovah. I would not be satisfied with meekly counting this as an agreement, if my neighbor did not insist that his merely dividing Jehovah into Persons did not interfere with His essential unity. If this were a new controversy, the whole would be abhorrent. I would quote at once, and insist upon the great zeal of the Bible to cut off everything *like* division. " Hear, O Israel ; the Lord our God is one Jehovah" (Deut. vi : 4). But when, in the long controversy of ages, my neighbor tells me that all this has been considered ; when he takes the passage, " I and my Father are one" (Jo. x : 30), and calls my attention to the fact that " *one*" is neuter, and, therefore, merely means one substance, one essence ; and when he takes the opposite text, " Now a mediator is not a mediator of one, but God is one" (Gal. iii : 20), and says, True enough, the " *one*" is masculine, but it means one Person as Jehovah, referring to a different personality from that of the Trinity,—I decline debate; I take the man's theory as he holds it. I think it too long a path to weary him down on these isolated texts : but I take his theory : his theory is, There are three persons : he tells me it is consistent : I mean by that, that he professes to see a consistency between the absolute unity of God and three Persons : * and, therefore, I follow the plan that I have stated. I take the unity of God, and consider it a ground on which we both unite. And then I ask him to go further. And when he expounds to me that the Spirit of God is of one essence with the Father, I say, Beyond doubt,

* Though the Bible says, " There shall be one Jehovah, and his name one" (Zech. xiv : 9).

but beg him to leave this ground in which we both agree, and lead me to the ground in which I can Scripturally see the disturbance into different Persons.

§ 2. *The Unity of God's Person not Disturbed by Different Names.*

Of course he cannot do that on the basis of different names. If he quote the words, The Father and the Son and the Holy Ghost, no matter where it can be found, whether in gospel form (Matt. xxviii: 19), or priestly benediction (2 Cor. xiii: 14), it proves not a single thing. The exuberance of the East multiplies appellations. That their sense is different, affords no evidence at all. And a confirmation of this is, that nobody dreams so. The Mighty God, the Holy One of Israel, the King in Zion, and any unnumbered list, Jehovah, Redeemer, the Lord our Righteousness,—on any account of their number,—or on any account of their diversity of sense,—are no proof of a Trinity. There must be more special reasoning. For, thus far, all parties must agree; that the Holy Ghost, for example, as an appellation, is not to be set down as not an appellation for the Almighty, or to be set off to some distinguishable Person, except for special reasons different from the fact that it is a different name, or that it means differently from other words for the Most High.

Again we are in agreement, therefore. No man would take the words, Jehovah, and, the Lord Almighty, and, simply because they mean differently, conceive a hypostatic difference. We still have, therefore, the evidence unfurnished. If the Trinity is true, we are driving in all imaginary outposts, and taking the very wisest plan to shut it in its citadel, and make it tell its actual clue for its discovery in the Word of God.

§ 3. *The Unity of God's Person not disturbed by Emblems.*

It cannot prove itself by emblems—I mean by the mere fact of emblems.

If I read of the " arm of God," there is no reason that I should discuss it. There is no demand in the English, and none especially in the richness of the East, that I should even stop to notice it. The " hand of God," the " eye of God," the " foot of God," and a perfect wilderness of such expressions, require not a word of comment. I should only vex people by stopping to explain. If I should ask, Is the " arm of God"(Is. li : 9) the same as God, people would laugh at me; not that the question might not be answered, Yes, and No, but that when it was answered both ways, with every possible distinction, the very best mind would be less clear than it was at the beginning. All men understand such expressions. Trinitarians could make a list of them by hundreds; and they would never dream that they had reference to a Trinity. And if I were to read, " The word of God," they would agree with me—I am sure a fair Trinitarian would,—that the "*prima facie*" impression should be, that it is a mere emblem. He would admit that he must bring contrary evidence from otherwheres; and that the " finger of

God" is no less evidence of a divine Person, than "the word of God" (Ps. cvii: 20), if it is to be anything in the emblem itself that is to reveal to us the mighty difference.

§ 4. *The Unity of God's Person not Disturbed by His Holy Spirit.*

Here, then, we are confronted, in a way easy for the estimate of proof, by the mention of the Holy Spirit.

Let us proceed cautiously.

Imagine our reading of "*the Spirit*" for the first time.

To a Hebrew eye the word would be "*breath.*" We read it as "*spirit.*" We read it by a word that has strayed away from its sense. But the Hebrew had only partly done so. It was like a bird with the shell still partly upon its back. Therefore, when the Jew read about the "spirit," he was really reading about "breath"; and the word remained sufficiently often in its sense of "*wind*" (Gen. viii: 1), or in its sense of "*breath*" (Is. xxx: 28), to make him the exegete each time the word occurred. And, therefore, when he read of the Breath of God (Ps. xviii: 15), the most candid arguers must confess, that, even if it appeared to him as Spirit, and even if he had grown familiar with what is meant by the spirit of man, he would not be led, in the multiplicity of Bible emblems, to keep it out generically from the class of God's finger, or God's eye, or God's power, which are to be taken as they stand, without any reference at all to any Trinity.

When any violence is done to this, I mean to the simple stand that no doctrine of the Trinity is to be learned from emblems, see what a desperate work is made. The whole emblematic skies break into hypostatic differences. Listen to Cyprian. He says, "That Christ is the hand and arm of God." He finds it in Isaiah; "Is God's hand not strong to save? or has he made his ear heavy?" (Is. lix: 1). The singular thing is, that such men drop the "ear," and take the "arm," without the least logical remorse: just as modern Trinitarians drop the "finger" (Lu. xi: 20), and take the spirit (Matt. xii: 28), without the least halting at their implied equivalency. "Also in the same place, 'Lord who hath believed our report? and to whom is the arm of God revealed?' (Is. liii: 1): also in the same, 'All these things hath mine hand made' (Is. lxvi: 2): also in the same, 'O Lord God, thine arm is high, and they knew it not' (Is. xxvi: 1): also in the same, 'The Lord has revealed his arm, that holy arm, in the sight of all nations' (Is. lii: 10): also in the same place, 'The hand of the Lord hath done these things, and the Holy One of Israel hath shown them': Is xli: 20." (Cyprian, Vol. II. p. 101, Clark's Ed). This, of course, as a *reductio ad absurdum*, carries the war directly into the Trinity. The Valentinians furnished the like. They said that "*Arche** was a divine Hypostasis, distinct from the Father and the *Logos*" (Irenaeus, Haer. I: viii: 5). The Patristic view made it the "Divine Sophia" (Origen). Cyril made it the "Everlasting Father" (see Meyer on John i: 59). All which most distinctly

---

* "The beginning" (Jo. i: 1).

teaches; that there has been a tendency in the theologic world to do just what our fathers did with the wafer, that is, to exalt it into a mystery, and to make the simple utterance, "This is my body," imply a divine sense, utterly beyond the meaning of the emblem.

"Wisdom" is scarce so ripe an instance; for the majority of commentators cling to it yet. It is instructive in that respect. It is a myth in the transition stage between a superstition and more sound intelligence. The church, giving up the "*Arche*," and the church giving up the "Arm," and the "Hand," and, now, the church slowly giving up the hypostatic "Wisdom," and, let me add, giving up the wafer, and giving up the mystic baptism, may be a type of the church giving up the Trinity; and, therefore, this transition link, viz., the Divine *Sophia*,* may be looked upon with more concern, as showing how fast or how slow the church will change her theories in other Scriptures.

Look well, indeed, at this instance of wisdom. It is loaded with hypostatic appearances. "The Lord by wisdom hath founded the earth" (Prov. iii: 19). I hardly know how personification could have been carried further. "I love them that love me, and those that seek me early shall find me" (viii: 17). The *Sophia* leaps upon the throne of the universe. "I will pour out my spirit unto you; I will make known my words unto you" (i: 23). There is emptied upon it an exuberance of Eastern *prosopopœia*. And so, if we hypostasize anywhere, why not

* "Wisdom."

in this moving and speaking reality? And yet all the time, close under the eye of the church, and still unlistened to, are the most ample texts (Job xxviii: 28; Ps. cxxxvi: 5; Prov. iv: 5, 7), to show that wisdom is mere piety; that the Lord by wisdom has founded the heavens, just as he is righteous in all his ways; that "by me kings rule," just as justice and judgment are the habitation of a throne; and that, categorically, Wisdom *is* righteousness (Prov. i: 2, 3); a statement made just where it should be, at the opening of the Proverbs; but singularly overlooked in a false and ungrammatical translation.*

Emblems, therefore, are no evidence of a Trinity. And the abuse of emblems, made hypostatic and then universally recalled, will bring the church to this mind,—first, that there is a proclivity to typical mistake, and, second, that there should be the most inexorable care, to sift the evidence before we divide the Deity.

§ 5. *The Unity of God's Person not to be Disturbed by Grammatic Differences—and First, not by Differences of Person.*

Verging on to points where more special evidence is imagined, I think we may still maintain agreement with Trinitarians in saying, that differences of person, in a grammatic sense, are not to establish the Trinity. I know it has been imagined differently. I know that advocates of Trinitarian belief have said, that the Thou and the I and the He in the mouths of the Father, Son and Holy

---

* See Author's Commentary, Prov. i: 1, 2.

Ghost, in speaking of each other, betokened hypostatic distinction. I know that they have brought this into the forefront, and given it a place as though it were an irrefragable appeal. But did they really mean that this did anything more than merely match the facts? Did they mean that it established them? They can hardly have meant the latter; for the expression " Awake, O Sword, against my Shepherd" (Zech. xiii : 7), would then mean that the Sword was a separate hypostasis. Or the expression, " His arm shall rule for him" (Is. xl : 10) : or the expression, " Awake, O Arm of the Lord" (Is. li : 9). I do not deny that if there *be* Persons in the Trinity, then I, Thou and He would agree with the facts. But that is not the question. As there is man and God in Christ, I, Thou and He agree with the speaking of Christ, and communing in his human nature directly and perpetually with the Divinity that was within him. Such were not the points at issue. The points at issue are, whether God, outside of Christ, is so distinguishable into three hypostatic personages, as that the grammatic persons *prove* the hypostases, or that the I, Thou and He are actual evidence that there are three Persons in the Godhead.

And that they are not, take these texts, " Bless the Lord, O my soul" (Ps. ciii : 1). Does that prove that the soul and I are, in any sense, different? Take this text, " And then will I say to my soul, Soul, take thine ease; eat, drink and be merry" (Lu. xii : 19) Or take this, " My heart said unto me, Thy grace, Lord, will I seek" (Ps. xxvii : 8). " My soul, wait thou only upon the Lord, for my expectation is from him" (Ps. lxii : 5). See the force of my reasoning. It is, that if the Trinity were established, there are moulds of Scripture into which it would run, just as there are grammatic differences that agree with the idea, that a man was united with the Almighty. There are modes of speech that will fall easily into place, if it were found that a man and his soul could commune and hold intercourse together. But the proof of the original fact must be outside the grammar. I think we have swept our horizon on, and not as yet discovered a distinct article of proof, which, even an honest promoter of the Trinity would be likely to declare, could build, in its own strength, the smallest demonstration.

§ 6. *The Unity of God's Person not Disturbed by Differences of Gender.*

Now as to gender.

The argument here is twofold. First, it may be said, The Holy Ghost is neuter, and, therefore, so bold a severance proclaims something very distinct hypostatically. And, second, the Holy Ghost, though neuter, has the masculine pronoun, as though the divine text would take pains to intimate, that this Spirit, first hewn off by being neuter, should, nevertheless, be redacted into a Person, by force of the grammatic proof to be gathered from the pronoun.

Now this is somebody's proof; and there ought to be somebody willing to stand for it. And when somebody is willing to stand for it, he ought really to stand. Theology, among all possible schemes, ought to retrench its arguments, till it gets down to those which it can possibly vouch: and when it has arrived at them, it ought to stand by them. It ought to be willing that they should stand distinct; and, when they distinctly and by their own merits fail, it ought to give them up; and not carry into the war crippled and everywhere defeated evidence.

For, look now at these genders. In the first place, the Holy Ghost is found to be neuter, because, in many a text, it is really neuter; that is, it verges gradually from meaning God, through all possible shades of thought, till it means a creature. This was the secret of the Arian mistake. There were so many passages inapplicable to the Almighty, that they seemed forced into some other scheme; and, therefore, conceived of the Highest of the Creatures, instead of that Holy Ghost which, in most of the texts, was nothing but the Almighty. Why can we not resort to a simpler exegesis? The arm of the Lord, or the power of the Lord, or the voice of the Lord, are nothing, *qua essentia*, but God Himself. They might, or might not, be neuter, just as it might happen. They might, or might not, in rhetoric, be convertible with the name of the Almighty. But who would require that some nurse should go with him, like a Duenna with a child, to pencil the shades of meaning? and who would not be pestered, if, instead of being left to his own quick conceptions as he reads, he were followed by somebody, incessantly to explain how much the hand or the foot or the breath of Jehovah was convertible with Himself, or how far it was to be considered distinct, and was subjective or resultant in its character?

So, now, in the instance of the Spirit. Sometimes it is plainly God; as where it says, "Now the Lord is that Spirit"(2 Cor. iii: 17). Sometimes it is plainly man; as where it says, "Every spirit that confesseth" (1 Jo. iv: 2). And between these there are all grades. It is a mere question of rhetoric, how quenching the Spirit (1 Thess. v: 19), or sowing to the spirit (Gal. vi: 8), or "your love in the Spirit" (Col. i: 8), or lusting against the spirit (Gal. v: 17), or joining to the Lord in one Spirit (1 Cor. vi: 17), or standing fast in one Spirit (Phil. i: 27), or worshipping God in the spirit (Phil. iii; 3), or the ornament of a meek and quiet spirit (Jas. iii: 4), may, or may not, refer to God, or to God subjective in the soul; that is, to the soul itself imbued with the grace of the Most High.

Undoubtedly the whole emblem, God's Holy Spirit, ought to keep near, for its exegesis, to the idea of a breath. When we say, God is a Spirit, we wander a little. God is not a breath. God is the most solid of all subsistencies. When we say, God's Spirit is himself, we talk more rationally. It is like saying, God's power is himself; or God's arm, or God's word is but himself acting or uttering his voice. But when we say, God is a Spirit, it is like saying, God is an arm or a shoulder. It is not a natural expression; and, therefore, let me say just here, It is no where found in the word of God. Christ says to the woman of Samaria, "The true worshipper shall worship the Father in spirit and in truth" (Jo. iv: 23).

And then he adds, "spirit is God" (v. 24). This passage has been wonderfully perverted. Middleton has helped the delusion by saying that the article betokens the subject (Chap. iii: s. 4, § 1). I will not dwell upon this. Winer has amply refuted it * (Gram. § 18, 7). Suffice it to say, The order is given in the Greek. And it is not, " God is a spirit," which would be an unprecedented sentence; but, "spirit is God;" that is, the worshipping seat in man is conscience, which is the voice of the Almighty, that is to say, the spirit which is bred within him of God. "Spirit is God;" and, therefore, "they that worship him, must worship him" in the God-part; that is "they that worship him, must worship him in spirit and in truth" (v. 24).

Returning to this passage at another stage of our inquiry, I say, There is plenty of reason why Spirit should be neuter; first, and very prominently, because it happens to be neuter, *i. e.*, the word, and, second, because it is used in so many subjective ways, the disseverances of which are to be made by the simple reader.

So much for the first argument.

Now, for the second.

We meet the second by an immediate denial.

The first argument was, that Spirit, being neuter,

---

* I do not mean that Winer, either here or in Jo. i: 1, translates as we do; but I mean that he refutes Middleton's rule. So do Glassius and Rambach. See also Röhricht in Jo. i: 1. See, moreover Middleton himself; who does not make the rule absolute; but states, with great reasonableness, why the subject should *usually* have the article; reasons which throw their strength the other way in the instances with which we are at present concerned.

it was very different from the Father; a very good
Arian argument; but not very good for the orthodox. The second argument was, that, though neuter, it drew to itself the masculine pronoun; an argument that I heard the other day in a sermon; an argument not conclusive, if it were correct; but an argument singularly unhappy, inasmuch as it is King James that puts-in the masculine (e. g. Jo. xiv: 17 xv: 26). With an uniformity that would be hard to equal, the Greek *pneuma* is every where followed by neuters (Mar. i: 10; Jo. vi: 63; xiv: 17; Gal. iv: 6); and almost the only places where it varies, is where the emblem has been kindled into a higher glow by the use of the word Comforter, which *is* a masculine, and which once or twice (Jo. xv: 26; xvi: 13, 14) draws the Spirit into its gender, and creates the cases, which are the sole warrant for any such thought of change.

The change of the neuter, therefore, in the common noun *pneuma*, is anything but an argument; in the first place, because it would be but a higher instance of personification, and, in the second place, because it does not occur, at all in the measure, or at all under the circumstances, which, as an argument it would lead us to suppose.

§ 7. *The Unity of God's Person not Disturbed by Difference of Number.*

Number possesses advantages over person and over gender if anything could be made out of these grammatic differences. Number stands out in actual letters. For example, God (Elohim) is in the plural.

There is no blinking the fact of this unnatural name; and no resisting the conclusion that it must have some peculiar explanation. If it were but once, or if it were but of one name!—but sometimes Maker (Ec. v: 7; xii: 1), sometimes the Most High (Dan. vii: 18), oftener Lord (*passim*), are presented in the plural. And, then, there are whole sentences; " Let us make man" (Gen. i: 26): " Let us go down" (xi: 7): " Let us confound their languages" (ib.); " Let us make man in our image, after our likeness" (i: 26): " Behold, the man is become as one of us" (iii: 22): sentences that have been eyed curiously for hundreds of years; and that were looked at very closely by the schoolmen, as betokening a Trinity.

But now, as of all other rights that can be pled, certainly it may be pleaded that orthodox men shall choose whether these do, or do not, support what has been imagined.

Strange to say, here has been a difference.

Men have found it so easy to explain these plurals. Some have said, they were regal plurals, as when a king, or high officer of State, said "we" or "us." Some said they were plurals of honor (Gesenius, *Lex*:), a form quite familiar in other passages of Scripture (Gen. xxxix: 2, Prov. i: 20; xxiv: 7). Some said, they were the remains of polytheism, and habits bred upon speech by a plurality of Deities (Naegelsbach, *Heb. Gram.*). Some said they were comprehensive terms, intended to associate the angels (Philo); or intended to gather in all traits, like *shamayim* for heaven, or like *mayim* or *hayim* for water or life (Ewald, Dietrich). This last is probably the best solution. But our object is altogether in the way of argument. What it means, or what it does not mean, does not concern us, unless it is insisted that it means the Trinity. So that we have a right to ask, Is this the case? Great numbers have utterly abandoned it. So has Hengstenberg. So have the great mass of the learned. So have nearly all who are not, in a conglomerate way, going back to all traditional arguments. I merely ask, Am I to answer it? If I am not, I shall leave nothing posted in my rear. If I am, I simply resort to this:—I say, The most devoted Trinitarians admit that it can prove nothing by itself; and I explain, Not simply because it can mean so many things; but because it would mean too much; for if God hypostatically differs, because he is spoken of in the plural, then the Spirit hypostatically differs, and wisdom hypostatically differs; that is to say, the Spirit must be in seven persons, because he is spoken of as "the seven Spirits of God" (Rev. iii: 1), and "wisdom" must be divided similarly, because it is stamped with the same mark; that is, it has the same plurality of name, and that by no unfortunate accident of manuscript revelation (Prov. i: 20).

Number, therefore, can do nothing for a Trinity. Nor can case.

§ 8. *The Unity of God's Person not Disturbed by Difference of Case.*

Jehovah is often in the nominative where some other name of God appears in the accusative, and where action and reaction are insisted upon as showing that the Actor and the Acted-on must be in a distinct hypostatical condition.

But now, boldly,—God sent his truth (Ps. xliii: 3; lvii: 3). Does that legitimately mean that God, and the truth that he sent, are different agencies? God sent down his power (Acts x: 38). Does that mean what the argument would imply? I know that, if there be a Trinity, there is no contradiction at all in such expressions; and, therefore, two things must be kept in mind,—what a sentence will tally with, and what it will prove. It will tally with the Trinity to say, God sent forth his word (Ps. cvii: 20). But to take two texts, and say, Send down thy power, and, Send down thy Spirit; and say, One proves a Trinity, and the other does not; or to say, Send out thy word (Ps. cxlvii: 18), and " Send thine hand" (Ps cxliv: 7), and insist, One is hypostatic in its very self, and the other not hypostatic in the least, but visibly and *in se* not so, is trifling with human thought. " Went not mine heart with thee?" says the prophet (2 Ki. v: 26). A book thronged with the exuberance of the East, that is said to have a clue, in its figures, by which they separate themselves in instances like these, is made to injure itself with the wise. Let us have the real proof for what we are to believe. For I beg an eager scrutiny thus far, that I may not leave upon the field anything valid, but may keep within the narrowing line everything that can be gravely introduced to support the Trinity.

§ 9. *The Unity of God's Person not Disturbed by Any Other Differences.*

I suppose many a grave man, if he did me the honor to read what I have written, would settle back upon his creed, and say, This is trifling, after all. All this may be honest; but yet it has the effect of a trick.

The scheme is one for matching Scriptures. Scriptures being found that uphold the Trinity, they are counterfeited; that is, like ones are put forward as meaning the same; and as neutralizing all the others. There is a ghastly cousinhood to those feats in Egypt. Aaron came forward, in the majesty of truth, and, the magicians, they also did likewise with their enchantments; for they also cast down their rods, and they also became serpents. I feel uneasy, myself, in every word I set forth. And when I hear Paul casting this old account into a form of general apostacy, and hear him say, " As Jannes and Jambres withstood Moses, so do these resist the truth," I wince under the picture. For this is indeed my very method. My challenge is, Bring on your sentences, and I will match them. And this springs from a persuasion that it can be done. All my study of the texts leads me to believe, that there is not one that usually supports the Trinity, that cannot be matched by another; and that the Father and the Son and the Holy Ghost cannot be presented in any form in the Bible, that cannot be matched by some other form: the form, seeming to imply a Trinity, having the implication taken out of it thus,—that (always reserving the peculiarities of the Son) the Father, the Word and the Holy Spirit can always be expounded by the light of other passages, where the conjunction is similar, but where the Lord of hosts and the Mighty One and the Holy One of Israel, or like groups, cannot be considered in any triune relation.

There is nothing, therefore, but to advance.

Grammatic case, grammatic gender, grammatic person, grammatic number, and all grammatic differences, have been appealed to. Now let us have everything else. What are the special forms of proof on which the ages could have built so great a doctrine?

1. It may be said, The Holy Ghost stands out so as an agent! Personification may answer in poetic writing : but in the most lengthened prose, and in so many and such varied portions of revelation, the Holy Ghost is talked of as so strictly a person, that the style of the thing, rather than any distinctive case, betokens the cause of the belief of Christendom.

But be careful! Who is denying that the Holy Ghost is a person? That may be a good argument against the Arian, and against similar mistake. Our very claim is, that the Holy Ghost is a Person ; and that he is only One Person. Our doctrine is, that the Spirit is God. When, therefore, it is said, that the Holy Ghost spake (Acts xiii : 2), or that the Holy Ghost came on them (Acts xix : 6), or that the Holy Ghost did any act or work (Acts x : 44 ; xvi : 6 ; xx : 28 ; Rom. v : 5), we do not object, in the least. What does it prove? It proves that the Holy Ghost is a person. We *claim* that the Holy Ghost is a person; and we aver, that not one of these passages shows that he is any separate person from the Word or the Father.

2. The same is our conclusion from his being an object of worship (Is. vi: 3, 9; cf. Acts xxviii: 25). We are right in riveting the proof. If any man has it, let him produce it. We are reasonable in tracing the evidence along. And if we say, This is not evidence; and this is not evidence; nor this,—we are, in method, right. Nay, we are doing a favor to the truth, if we cut off meaningless appeals, and bind the Trinity down to its actual demonstrations.

3. But it may be said, Whole passages are demonstrative of what we are seeking. It may not do to quote, "The Holy Ghost spake" (Acts xxviii: 25), and then say, that, by the force of that one expression, there is some other Person than the Father; or that, because that Person is worshipped (Jo. iv: 24), and prayed to (Ez. xxxvii: 9),—that therefore he is a distinct hypostatic divinity; but when a whole narrative occurs; as, for example, like this, "If I go not away, the Comforter will not come unto you; but, if I depart, I will send him unto you: and when he is come he will reprove the world of sin and of righteousness and of judgment:" or, when we read, "And whosoever speaketh a word against the Son of Man, it shall be forgiven him; but whosoever speaketh against the Holy Ghost, it shall not be forgiven him" (Matt. xii: 32): or, when we read, that certain worshippers did not so much as know that

there was a Holy Ghost (Acts xix : 2), there is a cast about this that should operate differently from any isolated text, and a persistence of using a name, that seems to imply a more than mere rhetoric for the Almighty.

But why?

Let me press the point just there.

Solomon breaks out in the most remarkable personification of wisdom. He follows it, chapter after chapter. He harps upon it ; till we should suppose he had worn out the figure, if persistence is any sign that that could be done. The Spirit is nothing, in elaborate drapery, to the personification of wisdom. I beg a close inspection of the comparison involved. Wisdom ; which has not an advantage like the Spirit ; because it is not really a personal Deity,—nevertheless builds houses, and shelters guests (Prov. ix : 1). It actually builds for the Almighty (Prov. viii : 27, 30) · and props kings upon their thrones (v. 16). And if any one says, Yes, because it is a Person, I hail that as confirming my demonstration. Wise persons believe that it is not a person ; and if the *prosopopœia* is piled so high that it seems so, it is all the better argument. If Paul talks so of Sin (Rom. vii : 13) that she seems like Milton's Goblin, scaly and venomous before us, I think, with the superior advantage that the Comforter is really a Person, we can be spared from admitting, from the text, that it need be a Person separate and distinct from the Father.

But it may be said, That strange expression,— They did not so much as know that there was a Holy Ghost ! (Acts xix : 2). Well ; let us look at that.

Will the Trinitarian really admit that they did not know that there was such a Person? If he does, then the world-wide doctrine, such as he believes the Trinity to be, was not known to the Jews of Ephesus. That is unreasonable enough. But then, another consequence. There could not have been a Holy Ghost. There could not have been one, because there was none in the days of our Saviour: and an eternal Spirit must have existed always. And there was none in the days of our Saviour, because we are distinctly told, that " there was no Holy Spirit yet,* because that Christ was not yet glorified" (Jo. vii: 39). We have got, therefore, to retrace our steps; for this, of course, no man will endure.

What then is the meaning?

We have already explained, that Spirit is often subjective. Indeed, we have shown that it is more and more subjective; until it settles, at last, to be no more than conscience. When, therefore, John said, that there was not yet any Spirit (Jo. vii: 39), he meant, undoubtedly, the great promised work of the Spirit. And when the Ephesians said, that they did not so much as know that there was a Spirit, they meant his promised work (Acts xix: 2). They, no doubt, had fruit of the Spirit; but they were speaking comparatively, just as when Paul said, Christ sent me not to baptize (1 Cor. i: 17). So that the whole meaning was, that the great Pentecostal blessing had not dawned upon their minds.

But here now a very strong argument! Why use

---

* "Given" (E. V.), as will be seen, is in Italics. The Greek, as to the point involved, is, in each case, precisely similar.

such language? If there was a Holy Ghost separate and distinct from the Father, and such a hypostatic Personage was a great reality of the gospel, John would have been very shy of using such language. Such slight considerations have often the force of demonstration. If God were not in Persons, but were simple; if he were not hypostasized literally, but were Spirit or Word rhetorically, or as the case may be, the pen would not hesitate to write, "There was as yet no Holy Ghost": but if the Trinity is true, it would seem unreasonable and wrong, and, in fact, rhetorically impossible, to write in one of our theologies, for example, that there was at any given time no Holy Ghost.

In respect to the unpardonable sin—what is it? If the Son of Man appear as an outward revelation; and if the Holy Ghost be felt as an inward influence, —I can understand the sentence at once. If any one speak a word against the Son of man, he merely denies a doctrine, or is found denouncing God as outwardly revealed. But if any man speak a word against the Holy Ghost, the implication is, that he is resisting inwardly; that is, that he is doing violence to conscience; that is, that he is trampling the Spirit of grace, which is God at work upon his mind.

The passage, therefore, is adverse to the doctrine of the Trinity. If God be in three persons, the speaking a word against Father, Son or Holy Ghost would seem equally offensive. Indeed, a speaking against the Father would seem to be the most bold. Each would have its point of heinousness. The Father, as the great King and Judge; the Son, as having tabernacled in clay, and as having been the price-affording strength of the obedience and the ransom; or the Holy Ghost, as our Sanctifier, would be each most reverend and great; and that would be a useless mystery that would seem to erect the one over the other. But explain the whole as I have said, and mystery vanishes. Jesus Christ can be looked at in his humanity. Jesus Christ, in his humanity, was an outward thing, and could be looked at like the Bible. Jesus Christ, like the Bible, could be rejected by a profound mistake. But Jesus Christ, in the Spirit; or, as we could then expound it, the Father in the Spirit; or, to speak still less figuratively, the Great God operating as a holy breath,—is a Monitor inside the heart. It is a monition that has gained access to the spirit. It is a conviction that has passed out of the category of mistake, and become inwrought in the soul. Then to quench it, is insolent wrong. And hence the intimation, that, whereas the susceptibilities of life can be so worn away, that, according to the rules of grace, a man is past feeling (Eph. iv: 19), so this process may be hastened, and a violence to the inward light sovereignly poured down, may grieve the Almighty to depart, and may finish, at a stroke, the possibilities of salvation.

Glance, therefore, at the argument. We are not denying the personality of the Spirit; nor his divinity; nor a meaning in the name. We pray for the Holy Ghost. We depend upon the Holy Ghost. And without this blessed Monitor, we are lost forever. His work is a work of the new birth, sanctification and calling into life. All this we delight in

We only say, It is God thus beautifully described. When he descended in cloven tongues, of course nobody believes that God was a fire. When he dwelt as a Shekinah, he was not the luminiferous ether. When he descended on Christ, he was only in the *form* of a dove. And, so, I carry what is spectacular to a still higher degree. I hold the Holy Breath to be only God (2 Cor. iii : 17). When I pray that it be poured out, I pray for God. When waiting for its coming, I wait for the Almighty: and for all-abounding reason; for, as we have carefully seen, gender and number and case have all been appealed to, and every opportunity has been given for each imaginable trace, and no footstep has been seen of a divided Deity.

4. One thing yet remains, and that is the testimony of believers. I value this. In vital matters the testimony of believers is unquestionably infallible. But that is the very question. Is this a vital matter?

"The people of God have always regarded the Holy Spirit as a person. They have looked to him for instruction, sanctification, direction and comfort. This is part of their religion. Christianity (subjectively considered) would not be what it is without this sense of dependence on the Spirit, and this love and reverence for his person. All the liturgies, prayers and praises of the Church are filled with appeals and addresses to the Holy Ghost. This is a fact which admits of no rational solution, if the Scriptures do not really teach that the Spirit is a distinct person. The rule, *Quod semper, quod ubique, quod ab omnibus*, is held by Protestants as well as by Romanists. It is not to the authority of general consent as an evidence of truth that Protestants object, but to the application made of it by the Papal Church, and to the principle on which that authority is made to rest. All Protestants admit that true believers in every age and country have one faith, as well as one Lord and God" (Dr. Hodge's Sys. Theol. I. p. 526).

Notice the errors. First, faith in a Trinity has not been positively universal. Dr. Hodge would hardly deny the quality of faith to all Monarchians, or even to *all* Arian professors. Second, universal belief does not prove the truth of a doctrine; but it only proves it in case it is vital. Third, universal belief does not prove a faith vital. Witness the doctrine of the Mass, which has been universal in some ages, and is preponderant in this. The belief that it is vital does not make it vital, any more than it makes Jacobitism vital, or the right to persecute. And, therefore, fourth, the great flaw in this argument is, that it does not settle whether the doctrine is vital. If it is, I grant the Church has it; for if the doctrine is vital, it is only tantamount to owning that there is always a living church. But that it is vital because the church has it, I utterly deny; for the church has had masses, and auto-da-fés, and all sorts of barnacles, that have grown upon it as a penalty of iniquity.

There is no proof, therefore, thus far, that God exists hypostatically separated.

But, now, there is proof very positively the other way.

§ 10. *No Distinct Personality of the Spirit.*

Of course, theologians will not expect me to find expressions declaring, polemically, that there is no Holy Ghost. And the reason why not, will be altogether understood, when I declare, that there was no such doctrine. The East had no such polemic. The nearest we come to it is in the first texts of John, which, as we have already shown, were against the errors of the Platonists (Irenæus iii : 11). And, perhaps, prophetically, Christ had some inkling of the kind, when, after more than usual hypostatic expressions about the Spirit, he says, " The time will come, when I will no more speak unto you in Proverbs, BUT WILL SHOW YOU PLAINLY OF THE FATHER." In the main, therefore, we cannot hunt up positive denials; because our plea is, that the Bible is colorless of the Trinity; and, therefore, we cannot array it either for it or against it.

But, *incidentally*, there are singular proofs.

1. In the first place, there is no care at all about the names of the Almighty. If there were a Trinity, there would be some precision that exegetes had reached. Jehovists would have gained the day, or *Malachists*, sifters-out of the meaning of the " Angel." The scene in Isaiah (Chap. 6) is applied to Father (v. 1), Son (Jo. xii : 41), and Spirit (Acts xxviii : 25), with no possible order. We appeal to every principle of frankness, whether the scheme that makes these names rhetorical,* and makes them all descrip-

---

* Excepting always the Son.

tive, does not apply to the confusion of their use more happily than to distinct hypostases.

2. Second, the confusion of powers! God is said to create (Gen. i: 1); and Christ is said to create (Heb. i: 10); and so the Spirit (Ps. civ: 30). They all garnish the heavens, and work the works of the Great Builder, promiscuously together (Jo. v: 17). And this has been urged to prove that they are but "One Substance." But does it not go further, and hint that they are but One Person? Are they not, like the mason's tie, binding the wall, and bringing back these garnishings of speech to what our Saviour calls, a telling plainly of the Father?

3. Then we have the confusion of the Persons. We have the direct declaration, " Spirit is God" (Jo. iv: 24). Paul declares to us, " Now the Lord is that Spirit" (2 Cor. iii: 17).* In Matthew we are told, I cast out devils by the Spirit of God (Matt. xii: 28), and, in Luke, I cast out devils by his finger (Lu. xi: 20). We hear " of the Spirit and of power" (1 Cor. ii: 4). We hear, " The Holy Ghost shall come upon thee, and the power of the Highest shall overshadow thee" (Lu. i: 35). " Whither shall I go from thy

---

* We ask special examination for two texts, one in John, and the other in the Epistle to the Philippians. The one in John is translated, " For God giveth not the spirit by measure" (Jo. iii: 34, E. V.). Why not translate it, " For God, the Spirit, giveth not by measure"? The other passage reads, " Which worship God in the spirit" (Phil. iii: 3, E. V.). Why not translate that, " Which worship the Spirit God"? or, as the Greek is contested, and the reading, *theou*, is believed to be correct, why not discard Meyer's rendering, " Who worship in the Spirit of God," and fix on the more natural translation, " Who worship the Spirit of God"? The whole pneumatology of the Bible is worth a careful revision.

Spirit? or whither shall I flee from thy presence"? and Clement goes on with this passage, "If I ascend into heaven, thou art there; if I go away even to the uttermost parts of the earth, there is thy right hand; if I make my bed in the abyss, there is thy Spirit" (Chap. 28). The very Fathers seem not to have traced a Trinity. We hear them say, "The Word is the Spirit."* Hermas says, "I wish to explain to you what the Holy Spirit, that spake with you in the form of the church, showed you; for that Spirit is the Son of God" (*Pastor of Hermas*; Clark's Ed. p. 404). The Targumist renders Zach. vii: 12, "by his Word," instead of, "by his Spirit." And Hermas takes up the emblems at will, " No one shall enter into the kingdom of God, unless he receive his holy name . . . Whosoever shall not receive his lips, shall not enter into the kingdom of God" (p. 416). We can multiply into any multitude these ignoring revelations. "In the Scriptures themselves the same work is often ascribed to God and to the Spirit of God, which led some, at times, to assume that these terms expressed one and the same thing; as the spirit of a man is the man himself. In the Scriptures, also, the terms Word and Breath (or Spirit) are often interchanged; and what in one place is said to be done by the Word, in another is said to be done by the Spirit. The *Logos* is represented as the life of the world, and the source of all knowledge; and, yet, the same is said of the Spirit. Paul declares, in one place (Gal. i: 12), that

* No one can examine Lightfoot, Vol. II. p. 520, without seeing that those attributes that are ascribed by the Targumists to the Word, are precisely those specifically belonging to the Holy Spirit.

he received the doctrines which he taught by the revelation of Jesus Christ; in another (1 Cor. ii: 10), that he was taught by the Spirit. Misled by such interpretations" [as Dr. Hodge thinks], "some of the Fathers identified the Son and the Spirit. Even Tertullian, in one place, says, ' *Spiritus substantia est Sermonis, et Sermo operatio Spiritus, et duo unum sunt*'."* (Hodge, Theol. I. p. 533).

Let us quote other Scriptures. Job says, " By his Spirit he hath garnished the heavens; his hand hath formed the crooked serpent" (Job xxvi: 13). The Psalmist says, " By the word of the Lord were the heavens made, and all the host of them by the Spirit (breath, E.V.) of his mouth" (Ps. xxxiii: 6). We are told of miracles by his finger (Lu. xi: 20), by his Spirit (Matt. xii: 28), and then, traversing both, of " miracles and wonders which God did by him," that is, by Christ (Acts ii: 22). We hear of the Spirit of God as tantamount to, and illustrated by, the spirit of man (1 Cor. ii: 11). We are wearying the reader. Our argument will be understood. It is not that the Trinity is guarded against in Scripture: the fact that it is in no way mentioned, is our most important proof: but now,—with this subsidiary consideration, that, if the Trinity had been intended to be revealed, it would never be traversed and cut to pieces by incongruous appellations.

4. Fourthly; the offices of the Persons are confused. The Father would seem preëminently the

---

* *Adversus Praxeam*, 15, *Works*, edit. Basle, 1562, p. 426 [" The Spirit is the substance of the Word, and the Word the operation of the Spirit; and the two are one thing"].

Person who elects us into life; and yet the Son says, "Ye have not chosen me, but I have chosen you" (Jo. xv: 16). Kindred things are said of the Spirit (Eph. i: 13; iv: 30). The great work of redemption is by Christ; and yet the Father, in actual prophecies of the Son, calls himself the "Redeemer;" and the Holy Ghost, preëminently the Sanctifier, does not monopolize that title in the least, but shares it, whenever it is rhetorically fit, with the Father, and with the God Incarnate (Jude 1, Eph. v: 26). We shall recur to this indifferency of title under another head (1 Chap. iii: § 13 *et al*). But, in the meanwhile, like the lines of the spectroscope, the evidence may seem slight, but it is determinate. It is impossible for one moment to suppose that God was eternally three, and that that threeness was so original and of course as to have penetrated into human consciousness: it is impossible that, as Dr. Hodge declares, " it underlies the whole plan of salvation, and determines the character of the religion (in the subjective sense of that word) of all true Christians:" that "it is the unconscious (*sic*) or unformed faith even of those of God's people who are unable to understand the term by which it is expressed:" that they "believe in God the Creator and Preserver, . . . and, therefore, of necessity, in a divine Redeemer, and a divine Sanctifier;" and that they should " have the factors of the doctrine of the Trinity in their religious convictions"*: (Dr.

---

* "It is not too much to say with Meyer (*Lehre von der Trinität*, i. p 42), that 'the Trinity is the point in which all Christian ideas and interests unite; at once the beginning and the end of all insight into Christianity'" (Hodge, Theol. i: p. 443).

Hodge's Theol. I: p. 443): I say it is utterly impossible to dream of such a thing,—if the Word of God, which I suppose Dr. Hodge, in spite of our "consciousness," will still admit must be the source of the doctrine, is so utterly careless to keep the great terms of the doctrine, Creator, Redeemer, and Sanctifier, at all apart, and that in the most critical revelations.

CHAPTER III.

GOD THE SON.

§ 1. *The Deity of the Son.*

BEGINNING on the plan that we have laid down, we seize first, as a fact in which we are all agreed, upon the Deity of our Redeemer. Nobody doubts it. The Trinitarian believes that the whole substance of God is present in Christ; and we believe, precisely in the same language. Nobody, at all engaged in this polemic, is concerned about the Deity of Christ; for that is settled. The question is, Is the Deity in Christ the Second Person of the Trinity, or the One Personal Jehovah; the degree and measure of his divinity, if there could be any conceivable difference, being rather against the Trinitarian: for the Trinitarian believes in but one of three Persons as in Christ, whereas we believe in the Sole Person of the Almighty as present in our Great Redeemer.

§ 2. *The Humanity of the Son.*

So of the humanity. The Trinitarian believes that there is one body and one soul, and that these in nature are distinct from the Godhead. He believes in a finite body and in a finite reason; and, though there is a great deal of crude thinking about Emmanuel, yet, when put to his proofs, he believes that this finiteness remains, and that, this moment in heaven, there is a soul, one with the Deity, which is ignorant, —that is to say, unspeakably wise in comparison with what it was on earth (Phil. ii: 9), but still a soul; for the Trinitarian believes that Christ is "very man" as well as "very God": and, therefore, that the man should become God transmutedly, so that the faculties of the man should become the faculties of the Almighty, our brethren would be just as averse from as we are, and from the same articulate reasoning.

The humanity, therefore, is at rest between us.

§ 3. *The Begetting of the Son.*

The begetting of the Son is more agreed in than we would at first imagine.

It is true that we are coming, here, to the most violent differences.

But the begetting of the Son, in one distinct form of it, we would describe alike.

If I were to quote the passage, "Thou art my Son; this day have I begotten thee" (Ps. ii: 7), there are very few people that would say, with some, "Thou art my Son; this day art thou my Son" (Hodge, Theol. Vol. I. p. 475), as though it were a mere asseverance that thou art my Son at any and every period. Nor are there many that would say with others, Thou art my Son; I am he that have begotten thee.

(J. A. Alexander, Acts xiii: 33). These strained overcomings of the meaning are offensive to the most. But most exegetes, in good Saxon way, will admit that it refers to a temporal begetting; and will resort to the suggestion of Dr. Hodge, that there may be two begettings (Theol. Vol. I. p. 474). This, as will be seen, will analyze our subject. We will take the second begetting as a thing in which we are all agreed, and get that fixed first. And then we will go to the first, and, having stripped away all the passages that belong to the second, we will press the argument, that there are no such passages to substantiate the first as are worthy of the least consideration.

And, in regard to the second, Gabriel gives the best account of it. " The Holy Ghost shall come upon thee, and the power of the Highest shall overshadow thee; therefore, also, that holy thing which shall be begotten, shall be called the Son of God" (Lu. i: 35). This testimony might seem to be confused in the Acts of the Apostles (xiii: 32, 33), where this begetting is spoken of in connection with Christ's being "raised up again" (E. V.); but Dr. Hodge agrees that "again" is an interpolation (p. 475). The Greek means that Jesus was "raised up." We believe that that means more than a mere birth.* But Dr. Hodge's interpretation is enough for our present argument. He concedes that the birth may be alluded to in the expression, " this day." And, now, as the expression occurs four times in the Bible (Ps. ii: 7; Acts xiii: 33; Heb. i: 5; v: 5), we have that much attained at least: Trinitarians confess that,

* See the Treatise, " *Was Christ in Adam*" ?

"This day I have begotten thee," may refer to the birth of the Redeemer.

But they say, There was another birth, also; and that eternally of God. Now we desire the passages. It speaks of the first begotten of the Father. But, of course, that we hold ourselves. That was the child begotten of Mary's womb. There was no son like that Son. All other sons were shadows; and therefore the expression, "The only begotten Son of God."

Moreover, "in (by, E. V.) him were all things created" (Col. i: 16). We are to come to that hereafter (§ 11). When he was born, all things were born. That is, the shape of the universe so hung upon him, that not only did the Divinity that was in him make the universe, but it was made "in reference to him" (*eis*, Col. i: 16), as well as "by him." And, therefore, we are told that "in him all things stood together" (v. 17). Christ was not born as soon as the universe was born "in" him: that is, the whole plan of it took color from his advent. All the pardons of it were built upon him. All the government of it was to be laid upon him. The central kingdom of it was to be man's commonwealth (Heb. ii; 8). And, therefore, it was eminently true, that "in him were all things created," and that he was "the first born of every creature."

Under this head of "begetting," let the Trinitarian produce his arguments.

If he says, He was the "first begotten of the dead" (Rev. i: 5), that of course is in our favor, for an eternal begetting did not, of course, bring him out of a charnel-house; and that, therefore, helps our view; for it obtrudes another passage, confessedly applied to time; fixing this word "begotten" in connection with our Redeemer.

§ 4. *The Son and the Spirit.*

And while we are on the subject of the "begetting," let us trace the connection with it of the Spirit.

Listen to Gabriel: "The Holy Ghost shall come upon thee" (Lu. i: 35).

Christians are said to be begotten of the Spirit (Jo iii: 5).

Now, this lowering of the description to the case of man, does not make the Trinitarian averse to applying it to the Messiah.

He will confess that the "*Theanthropos*" was begotten of the Spirit.

See, now, what then he must embrace: first, that there was a true body; second, that there was a reasoning soul; third, that there was a Holy Ghost settling upon the Virgin Mary, and entering the child at his conception, as the great inspirer of his human life; fourth, a Second Person of the Trinity; and, fifth, a plenary God, that is, both Son and Spirit, possessing the plenary Deity, because being "the same in substance equal in power and glory."

Now, where is the proof of all this? The angel Gabriel seemed to say quite the opposite; for he stated the simple fact, "The Holy Ghost shall come upon thee." Why did he not speak of the Logos? Why is there no *soupçon* of a Second Person? Why did he exclude the Great Mystery? It may be said, He was not giving all the facts. Then why did he profess to? He said in the most oracular way, "The Holy Ghost shall come upon thee;" and then, fixing the doctrine for all time, he says, "Therefore—" and we can hardly suppose that he would tell a part of the reality—"Therefore," you a poor Israelite, and he a child in a cradle; you simply overshadowed by the Spirit, and he with a body and a mere rational humanity—"Therefore,"—as though, on a brief visit from the heavens, and on the brink of the most important of created histories, he would tell, at least, the most illustrious reality of the case,—"Therefore, that holy thing that shall be begotten, shall be called the Son of God."

I think, therefore, we may press two things, and urge a friendly answer; first, why was he to be "called the Son of God," at all, for any event in time, and not rather from his eternity's begetting? and, second, why was he "called the Son" for the overshadowing of the Holy Ghost, and not rather for the entrance of the SON, there being by that earlier name a Second Person in the Divinity, whose actual entrance into the man would be, as the Trinitarian would declare, the cause for his being the Son of the Almighty?

It will be noticed that a recoil of the question, and a demand how *we* get over the difficulty, would give us the most favorable chance for explaining the simplicity of our system. The five discordant things give us no confusion. We fold them up like a telescope. The (1) soul and the (2) body; they are the man. The Trinitarians will agree with us there. The (3) Spirit and the (4) Word and the (5) Deity: they are the God. When Gabriel said, "The Holy Ghost shall come upon thee," he was expounding the nature of Emmanuel. Did I believe that the Holy Ghost was one Person, and the Word another, and a Godhead comprehensive of both, I would be all at sea; but believing that Gabriel chose for his rhetoric the image of a Breath, and brought with him the title of a Spirit out of the vocabulary of heaven, I am at no loss at all. He simply meant, God shall come upon thee; and he confirms that by the synonym, "the power of the Highest:" and we have no room for confusion; for, in this way, he was announcing at once, God as tabernacling with clay.

§ 5. *The Son and the Father.*

It will be noticed that our blessed Redeemer never speaks of a Son as tabernacling with him. He never speaks of a Second Person. And, if that is considered as taking advantage of a something which is in modern speech, he never speaks of anything answering to that. He enters into long metaphysics in respect to his person (Jo. Chaps. v—xvii); but he never dreams of a hypostatic subtilty. He always speaks of "God," or "his Father." This, we insist, is an enormous evidence.

Think of it.

He often speaks as a man,—"I thirst" (Jo. xix: 28), or, I hunger (Lu. vi: 3), and he often speaks in ways which can only be understood if we suppose him as separating his divinity from his humanity (Jo.

v: 19, 30 ; viii: 28). In these views he speaks of his Father; but he never speaks of—what shall I say? There is no *Person* that can afford us a name outside of the One Divinity. All this is inexpressibly unlikely. Thirteen chapters in the heart of the Evangelist (v—xvii) discuss the Redeemer in the most unexpected ways. He says, " I and my Father are one" (Jo. x: 30). He says, " He that hath seen me, hath seen the Father" (Jo. xiv : 9). He says, " As the living Father hath sent me, and I live by the Father" (Jo. vi: 57). He says, The Father dwelleth in me, and I in him (Jo. xiv: 10 ; xvii: 21).

Now, Trinitarians agree here. They cannot change this language. They are reverent people, and would not desire to. And they have a meaning for it ; and would cheerfully agree that it expressed a relation with the Father. But will they go further, according to our plan of discussion, and we, having ventured where we agree, will they venture where we differ, and explain how Christ should refer everything to the Father, and that in critical passages where he is discussing everything that belongs to his subsistence?

" The Son can do nothing of himself, but what he seeth the Father do" (Jo. v: 19). " As the Father hath life in himself; so hath he given to the Son to have life in himself" (Jo. v : 26). " I can of mine own self do nothing" (v. 30).

Now, our distinct argument is, not, that Jesus Christ is not God ; for we hold that he is, in common with the Trinitarians ; not, that he can do nothing of himself: for we hold that he can, when he speaks as the Most High: but that, when he is speaking in human weakness, and that when he is saying those things that account for his subordination in the Deity, such chapters about himself declare three things, first, that there is no ante-Marian Son, or he would sometime speak of him; second, that there is no ante-Marian *hypostasis* of any sort, or it would be brought into the philosophy of his case; and third, that there is no Father; that is to say, that there is no hypostatically separated parent, different from the One Almighty (Jo. xiv: 9).

§ 6. *The Son as Jehovah.*

Hence he is called Jehovah. Isaiah says, I have "seen Jehovah" (Is. vi: 5); and John says, "These things said Esaias, when he saw his [Christ's] glory, and spake of him" (Jo. xii: 41).

But when, under the enthusiasm of such a discovery, we hunt up the texts that will make it more complete, we may, for a time, sail in very tranquil seas, Paul confessing "that the Lord is Jesus Christ"* (Phil. ii: 11), and the writer to the Hebrews quoting a strong Jehovistic passage (Heb. i: 10, Ps. cii): but hardly have we settled our theory, before it is chopped into by all sorts of cross waves. For, in the first place, the Holy Ghost claims the name. "Well spake the Holy Ghost by Esaias" (Acts xxviii: 25); and when we trace the speaking, it is that spoken by Jehovah (Is. vi), and that which John claims for Christ (Jo. xii: 41), and that which, in this way, becomes a link bind-

* The English translation has it "that Jesus Christ is Lord."

ing the imagined Persons into One, rather than an authority giving an hypostasis to any one of them.

Matters grow worse as we read more generally. The Jehovist can make no stand at all. The confusion becomes complete, as we study more deeply. And, not only is Jehovah one of the universal names for Heaven's Majesty: but more than that: it defies hypostatical treatment: and, for this sharp reason; —that there are passages, where the term Jehovah is employed, where it is applied to One who is speaking at the very time of his Son, our Redeemer.

I think I am making myself understood. I say that Jehovah cannot be a name of Christ, except as Christ is our One God and Creator, because Jehovah is a name for One who actually speaks of Christ; as, for example, in Isaiah,—" Jehovah said, In an acceptable time have I heard thee" (Is. xlix: 8): or again, in the Psalms, " Jehovah said to my Lord" (Ps. cx: 1; see also Ps. ii: 7). That cannot be an hypostatic name which is applied to the Father as well as to the Son. And as it is applied also to the Holy Ghost (Acts xxviii: 25), it becomes a mason's tie to bind together the structures of rhetoric which the antiquarian, man, treats with hypostatical separation.

§ 7. *The Son as Sent.*

Passing on to more difficult details, it may be asked now, why is the Son spoken of as sent? If he was born of the Virgin Mary, and if his separate subsistence from God was only as a man, then all those expressions which speak of him as " coming" (Eph. iv: 10), and, above all, those which speak of him as on a mission (Mal. iii: 1–4), or as being "sent" (Jo. x: 36), would seem rhetorically unmanageable.

This has been an argument much insisted on. But why should the rhetoric be significant when the very same is applied to John? Jesus Christ himself says, "Scripture cannot go for nothing" (Jo. x: 35). We insist, therefore, upon a meaning. "There was a man sent from God whose name was John" (Jo. i: 6). Prophets were "sent" (Jer. vii: 25). In fact, where a man's whole message came from heaven, it was not unnatural to speak as though the whole person of the ambassador descended also. In Christ's instance, all that gave him life came down from heaven. But without going into the intricacies of his person, it is enough to remark, that, if he could say of his disciples, "As thou hast sent me into the world, even so have I sent them into the world" (Jo. xvii: 18), it cannot be much of an argument that makes the expression, "sent," or the corresponding rhetoric for his advent, stand as a token of hypostases in the Almighty.

§ 8. *The Son as Wisdom.*

Christ, as "Wisdom," we have already dealt with (Chap. II. § 4). And yet I think we ought to go further. The fact that the Redeemer was ever dreamed of: nay, what is far more than that, the fact that, among modern commentators, nine-tenths, without a shadow of a relenting, take the old view; that Solomon should be directed to state, Wisdom is righteousness (Prov. i: 2, 3), and yet commentators declare, No; it is the Redeemer; that he should say, "Wisdom is the principal thing: therefore get wisdom: and with all thy gettings get understanding" (Prov. iv: 7), and yet trusted scholars declare, Wisdom is a Divine Hypostasis (Glassius, Calovius, Bp. Hall, Bridges, Scott, *et al.*), is like Cyril saying that *Arche** was the Father; or like Philo saying that it was the *Logos;* or like the Valentinians saying, it was a new hypostasis (see Irenæus, Hær. i: 8: 5). We should not be content simply to deride it; but we should go further. We should say, Is not this a proof that the soul tends to an abuse of figures? that it tends, for example, to make Divinity of a wafer? and ought not these confessed hallucinations to make us very wary of our work, when we are turning " Word" or " Spirit" into hypostatic Deities.

§ 9. *The Son and the Logos.*

This query comes directly into place when we take up, as we intend next to do, the doctrine of the Logos.

The doctrine of the Logos, we are frank to admit, is one of the strong points of the Trinity.

Would it not be fair, first of all, to ask, whether there is any argument for it in the Old Testament Scriptures?

The hypostasis of "Wisdom," we have seen, is well nigh universal. And "Wisdom," under the hand of a master, affords a most tempting chance for it. This figure stands out upon the canvas with most marvellous life. She speaks like a Deity. " I love them that love me." And, when she says, " I

---

* " The beginning " (Jo. i: 1).

also will laugh at your calamity," and when she says, " I have called, and ye refused ;" or when she says, " I will pour out my spirit upon you : I will make known my words unto you,"—it would seem easy, if the New Testament encouraged the idea, to make " Wisdom" Christ, and sweep all this beautiful speech into the volume of the gospel.

But when we are shown, by proof, that Solomon is meaning piety, I think we should allow more than all this drapery to fall, and should carry our sobered view *a fortiori* into the Logos.

For listen, now, to the theologians. One of the most distinguished boldly plants himself on this position. " In the Hebrew Scriptures the manifested Jehovah is called the Word of God, and to him individual subsistence and divine perfections are ascribed" (Dr. Hodge, Syst. Theol. Vol. i : p. 505). This, if it were launched at random, would be less to our purpose : but the texts are picked out (Ps. xxxiii : 6 ; cxix : 89 ; Is. xl : 8 ; Ps. cvii : 20 ; cxlvii : 18). Dr. Hodge has selected five of the Old Testament expressions. And I beg the reader to notice them closely ; for these are picked texts. " Wisdom" has passed, in all the splendor of her dramatic realness. And, now, these are to go by. I do not doubt that Logos has the more formidable claim. But where does it get it ? We are mustering everything in turn ; and, just now, are to be busy with the Old Testament revelation.

And, now, the first of Dr. Hodge's five texts is this ; " By the word of the Lord were the heavens made" (Ps. xxxiii : 6). The question is, whether that would teach a hypostasis any more than the "voice" of God, or the "name" of God. "By the word of the Lord were the heavens made, and all the host of them by the breath of his mouth." The question is, why one should be treated hypostatically, and not the other: and the question lies further, why translate the other word, "breath"? Why not translate it, "Spirit"? And if it be translated "Spirit," why give the same hypostatic work indiscriminately to both hypostases? and why, in fact, imagine hypostatic condition of either; I mean, in deference to the proof that can be extracted from this foremost one of the five selected passages?

The second is this, "Forever, O Lord, thy word is settled in heaven" (Ps. cxix: 89).

The third is this, "The word of our God shall stand forever" (Is. xl: 8).

The fourth is this, "He sent his word, and healed them" (Ps. cvii: 20).

The fifth is this, "He sendeth out his word, and melteth them" (Ps. cxlvii: 18).

These are the five texts.

I beg everyone to read them. And then I beg a verdict: whether "in the Hebrew Scriptures [these being the ones selected] the manifested Jehovah is called the Word of God, and to him individual subsistence and divine perfections are ascribed." And I ask this further verdict: whether, if this question be answered in the negative, the fact that these texts were ever thought of to teach a Trinity, is not an argument against it; and whether we do not start, in the consideration of the Logos, with some store of grounded motive to watch well the proof, before we think the Word of God is the base of any hypostatical relation?

If any antagonist declare, that the Jews looked very narrowly at these same passages, we shall begin there a series of remarks, which we shall depend upon entirely, to introduce us, in an intelligible way, into the New Testament testimonies. Beyond a doubt the Old Testament doctors of the law did deal with the Logos, and that in very extraordinary ways. Would it be unfair to ask, what was the propriety of what they did? As they resorted to very notorious expedients, the question has long ago offered itself, Were they right? or were they wrong?

And the world has answered.

They prepared important Targums; that is to say, they paraphrased the Old Testament revelation. These paraphrases were universally accepted; and, when Christ came upon the earth, they were in many synagogues, and the reading of the Targums was a thing familiar to Israelitish worshippers.

I beg you, pause at this. What the Targums taught, the Bible taught; so thought the Jews: and by that superstitious bent, notorious among the Rabbis, the Jews knew no difference; and what was surreptitiously brought into the faith, stood as well with vast herds of the people, if it was writ in the Targums, as if it was originally fixed as part of the word of the Almighty.

Now, one of the things superstitiously tampered with was "The Word of Jehovah." The Targums had multiplied it. Instead of the few cases incidental to an easy rhetoric, where the term, if it had been left, would have been easily understood, they made it memorable by writing it all the time. They cast out the word "Jehovah" two hundred times, and put in "the Word of Jehovah," with no other warrant than some growing and unquestioned superstition. This came down to New Testament times. Of course we have a right to be aware of it, and to watch it very narrowly. John, Irenæus tells us, wrote his gospel to oppose certain errors which he goes on to describe (Irenæus, III. 11). These Targums came into Africa. They were the treasures of the Ptolemaic time. They were coincident with the Septuagint. They mingled with the Greek literature. And, as the result, we have an understood form of faith. That is, it is a matter of history, that the Platonic Trinity, which is the first we read of as in the possession of Israel, wove itself upon this Targum frame; and now, as a thing actually confessed, produced a "WORD" which orthodox and errorists alike, confess was miserable superstition.

Irenæus describes it: "Monogenes* was the Arche,† but Logos was the true son of Monogenes. This creation, to which we belong, was not made by the primary God, but by some power lying far below him; and that [power was] off from communion with things invisible and ineffable" (Iren. B. iii: C. 11).

The Apocrypha, we ought long ago to have said, hypostasizing the "Word," and hypostasizing also "Wisdom," came out, on these superstitious grounds,

* "The Only Begotten." † "The Beginning."

in the strongest manner; and climbed up, partly by the help of such outspokenness, into unquestioned rivalry with the better canon. Philo came upon the scene. "Logos" became the *bête noir* of all Judaico-Ptolemaic thought. Philo ripened it into a system. Philo rooted it in the East. Though, the remark applied to him by Newman applies better perhaps to others his disciples, that, "associating it (the doctrine of the Logos) with Platonic notions as well as words, [he] developed its lineaments with so rude and hasty a hand, as to separate the idea of the Divine Word from that of the Eternal God, and so, perhaps, to prepare the way for Arianism" (Newman's Arians, p. 95).

Now John came. But before we seek light upon him, let us ask, What was this system, after all? It is impossible to say. Philo was full and explicit. But Philo was quickly departed from. There was no one system. But yet the tendency was this, to teach what was called a "Second God." The Logos was an emanation. It was not eternal; nor was it equal to the Father. Yet it was not a creature. It was intermediate, and subordinate; not brought into being by an act, but begotten; and yet not born from eternity, but, to express all in a single sentence, intermediate, and an emanation in time.

Undoubtedly this paved the way for Arianism; and John, when he came into the church, had to choose, whether he would ignore it, or refute it, or by a few strong words trample upon it; and this last, by the testimony of Irenæus, and as we tried to show in another part of our book, he took up his pen emphatically to do.

"In the beginning was the Word" (Jo. i: 1).

Let us now look at this somewhat more carefully. The Philonists taught that the "Logos" was an emanation in time. John denies this. He says, "In the beginning was the Word:" and, whatever he means by the "Logos," he sweeps, at one blow, all its intermediate nature. Then he goes further. He says, "The Word was *pros ton Theon;*" and, in Paul, *pros ton Theon*" twice means, "pertaining to" the Almighty (Heb. ii: 17; v: 1). It never means " with;"* I beg to insist upon this. The Greek " with" is entirely a different preposition. Then,— The Word was in the beginning, and it pertained to God. That is, whatever the Word might be found to be, it was always: it was not an emanation. Moreover it referred to God, like his " hand," or his " arm." And then, to put aside all doubt, " God was it;" just as we would speak of his " voice" or his " finger," if men began with them as a superstition. "In the beginning was the Word, and the Word had reference to God, and God was the Word:" and we have already shown how Meyer objects to this last, saying that *it would subvert the Trinity!* (see also Alford, *et al.*); and how Middleton has reigned for generations under the false syntactical pretence (see Gram. Chap. iii: s. 4, § 1) that the article before the " Logos" must necessarily reverse the Greek.†

---

* See note, I. Chap. V.

† On the contrary, the article is or is not before a word, simply for a purpose. It is not before it usually in the predicate, because the

To sum up; John does not discard the "Word." On the contrary; he uses it. It was used in the legitimate Scriptures. It had grown in the use of the people. It had been wonderfully abused. But it still means *God uttering himself:* and that he did in the Redeemer. And, believing that it was a graceful type, and believing that he must wrest it from its heresies, and uttering those sharp expressions in its case, he launches it again upon the page, alas! to be yet more misconceived, and to be made, like sentences of Christ (Jo. iii: 5; vi: 53; Matt. xvi: 18; Jo. xx: 23), the base of perpetuated superstition.

§ 10. *The Son and the Creation.*

Turning from the "Logos," which I ought to have said John returns to in its most ordinary signification* (Jo. xii: 48; xiv: 24; 1 Jo. ii: 14; Rev. xx: 4), I come next to that class of passages which speak of Christ as the Creator of the universe. Let me quote some of them. "By him were all things created" (Col. i: 16, 17). "By whom also he made the worlds" (Heb. i: 2). "Thou Lord, in the beginning,

predicate is usually generic, and not specific. But, in this case, it happens to be specific, and actually demands the article. We put it in the English. To get at our meaning we do not say, The God was Word, as we would say, "The knife was steel"; but we say, "God was the Word," just as in another case we say, "Spirit was God" (Jo. iv· 24; see the Greek); a case equally perverted and lost in the sense that was designed.

* Would there not have been more care about this, if John had really thought it was a Person of the Trinity? Would he not have been more saving of the term, and tried to keep it apart, just as we have said of Jehovah, if it had so rare a meaning?

hast laid the foundation of the Earth" (Heb. viii : 10). If Christ came to be, as a distinct actor upon the scene, only when he was born in Bethlehem, how possibly can we carve our way through these remarkable attestations?

And I ask, in the first place, How can anybody?

We believe that Jehovah was incarnate. That which was incarnate, therefore, made the world. We believe that Christ was born as a man. Christ as a man, never made anything. That, all will concede. We believe that Christ was of one substance with the Father. So do all of us. We believe that one substance made the world. So do all. We believe that the Three Persons made the world, if there are Three Persons in the Trinity. So do all (Eph. iii : 9; Heb. i : 10; Job xxvi : 13). We believe that there are not Three Persons in the Trinity, but that the One Person made the world. This is our sole point of difference.

Now if we thought as most persons think, we would take our stand upon this line, and say, Jesus Christ created the world, because he was incarnate Jehovah.

Why not say that?

It may be answered, because " by" or " through" Jehovah would not seem a significant revelation. Why not? as that very word is employed? (1 Cor. i : 9; Heb. ii : 10). At least, it may be said, God creating " by" God, or Jehovah " by" Jesus Christ, would not be a significant revelation, if Jehovah's One Eternal Person was all that was engaged in the creative act. Again I say, Wherein does the Trinitarian complain? for One Person creating "by" another Person, and One Person equal to that other Person, and that Person the same in substance, and all the Persons equally engaged in the work of creation, does not leave the Trinitarian much better, on a basis of grammatic sense, if *we* believe in the incarnation of our original Creator.

We are weak, however, in any such polemic, because we are fighting against our thought. We do not believe that it is referring to the original Jehovah. And when the apostle speaks of creating "all things by Jesus Christ" (Eph. iii : 9), I do not think the Trinitarian himself can exclude the Humanity from this assertion.

Let me explain.

If it were left peremptorily to decide whether God necessarily were a Trinity, because he created by Jesus Christ, I would say that One Person creating by Another Person, when both were one, and all shared in the creation, were a much more confused account than God creating " by " himself (Gen. xxii : 16; Heb. i : 3) : but as I believe that neither is the true solution, and both are alien from what is meant, I feel it far better to pay little attention to either, and go at once to that light which can be gathered from a more general survey of the sacred text.

I said, in treating of the Spirit, that it is in all degrees of subjectivity. When it says, The Holy Ghost spake (Acts xxviii : 25), it is hardly subjective at all. When it speaks of "a meek and quiet spirit" (James iii : 4), it is hardly Divine at all. Between the passages where it is so barely God as to retain little emblem of a "Breath," and those passages where it is so barely man as to retain little of the attitude of the Almighty, there are all degrees that intervene; and it has been a failure to keep up with the rhetoric, that has squared men down to Arian views of some intermediate Almighty.

Now, it is the same with Christ and the creation. Between the extreme of creation "by" Jehovah, and the extreme of creation "by" our fellow Man, there are all degrees of difference; and I wish to mention three, that almost stand by themselves with little other shading.

(1) For example, first, there is a passage in the Hebrews in which the Son is mentioned, and in which we read, " by whom also he made the worlds" (Heb. i: 2); and in which this Scripture is quoted in attestation: " Thou Lord in the beginning hast laid the foundation of the earth; and the heavens are the works of thine hands" (Ps. cii: 25). We turn to the Psalm, and it is throughout Jehovah. There is no sign of any discrepance of Person; and it is perhaps, beyond the majority of the Psalter, free of the Messiah. We bow our heads, therefore, to the fact, that the Jews referred it to the Messiah, or, at any rate, to the proof, that Paul, speaking by divine revelation, quoted it that way, and, therefore, that God's making all things by Christ is illustrated, in this particular case, by the fact, that Jehovah, who was incarnate in the Redeemer, originally and by himself made the worlds. This is the extreme in one direction; viz., he particle, "by," enfolding direct causation, as we now by all the Lexicons that it does in other parts

of the word of God (Rom. xi : 36 ; 1 Cor. i : 9). Then comes an intermediate case, where "by" is used for the norm or the rule. For example, in the instance of " Wisdom :" " The Lord by wisdom hath founded the earth ; by understanding hath he established the heavens" (Prov. iii : 19). To get rid of prejudice, let us take the second clause. " By understanding" cannot mean causally or efficiently ; it must mean modally ; and, therefore, we are given the warrant for God's doing " by" things that which he does causally and in himself ; and that of which the " wisdom" and the " understanding" express the mere normal relation.

Now, carry that to the instance of the " Word." "All things were made by him" (Jo. i : 3). Here the case is a little different. Here it is not mere " Wisdom." Here the rhetoric has been carried further ; and God has positively been announced to be the " Word." Still, I do not think *mere* causality is intended. If the Scriptures had said, " God is Love ;" and then gone on to say, God by Love made the heavens,—I would not think that it merely meant that God created them. I would think that there was more in the rhetoric. I would not think that it separated Love hypostatically from God, but that it was mere spoken common-sense ; mere Oriental effective speaking. I would not conceive that it implied a separate Person, but that God by the norm of his Love created all things under that modal inspiration.

So, now, of the " Word." I believe it is more rhetorical than " Love," because it is more the person.

It is more God actually uttering himself; and yet, for all that, when it says, "All things were made by him," I think it means more than that God made all things himself; and calls up the idea of a word, or universal decree, uttered from the beginning of time, "by" which, as the norm and also utterance of power, everything was made that was made.

(2) We mark this down, therefore, as the second shading of the representation.

(3) But there is a third. God from all eternity was not complete for the work of creation. He was complete in power. Give him the name of "The Word," and imagine that Word to be himself, uttered out in all his endless purposes: give him credit for all he is to be, and means to do, and then he is complete. But cut off from him future plans and the long-subsequent incarnation, and he can create nothing. I mean by that, he determined to build everything upon Jesus Christ. We see this in every part of the revelation. Christ was to be "head over all things to the church" (Eph. i: 22). And when we remember that God forgave for four thousand years, and ruled the world for four thousand years, and laid his plans before the creation of the stars and all upon Christ, I think we can begin to see what he means by creating "all things by Jesus Christ" (Eph. iii: 9). Moreover, considering that Christ was a man; considering that Jesus Christ was preëminently the Incarnate God; considering that he had no name like Jesus, before he was incarnate; and considering that Trinitarians themselves must believe that God out of Christ was a consuming fire; and that it was the suffering

and obedience of the man which it was necessary to build the world upon, as to the whole scheme of its creation,—I should think that even the Trinitarian would agree that there is a certain sort of sense in which God created the world by the man Christ Jesus.

Now, if there is any such sense at all, it is sufficient to be the whole sense. That is the argument we press. (1) "Thou Lord in the beginning": that is Jehovah; and means that Christ created all things, because he was Jehovah. (2) "All things were made by it" (Jo. i: 3). That is Jehovah too; but Jehovah as the manifested Word; and means that God created all things by one consistent self-uttering manifestation. But (3) "By him were all things created" (Col. i: 16); that is a much more complete idea; and means that God, without Christ, is imperfect; that is, that God, without Christ, is impossible; that life, without Christ, cannot be; that the world, without life, is a waste; that the universe, without Christ, is a failure; and therefore, that the Babe of Bethlehem, though a trifle (Is. xli: 24); though in himself a worm of the dust (Is. xli: 14); though an easy outbirth of God's omnipotence; and, therefore, sure to be;—nevertheless *had* to be; that is, that God was doing oceans of work without him, which depended upon him; that he was forgiving millions of souls; and that the whole shape of the creation was given by the man (who, nevertheless, was eternally God), who was born in a manger in the town of Bethlehem.

Now, that this was the meaning of the passages, we can tell by looking at them. Listen to the Apostle

Paul, "And to make all men see what is the fellowship of the mystery:" what mystery, except these unbased and unexplicated pardons?—but he goes on to explain: "which from the beginning of the world hath been hid in God:" now he is going to utter our very idea: "which from the beginning of the world hath been hid in God, who created all things by Jesus Christ" (Eph. iii : 9). These ideas are everywhere repeated. Paul says, "Who hath saved us according to grace, which was given us in Christ Jesus before the world began" (2 Tim. i : 9). Christ says, "Come ye blessed of my Father, inherit the Kingdom prepared for you from the foundation of the world" (Matt. xxv : 34). And Paul absolutely lays bare the whole rhetoric; for he speaks of such a case in Abraham, where God talks to an old shepherd, and calls a thing done, before there is even a gleam of it; and then says, "before him whom he believed, even God, who quickeneth the dead, and calleth those things which be not as though they were" (Rom. iv : 17).

Our doctrine, therefore, is, that Christ created all things. We agree with the Trinitarian that he is God, and, as God, built the universe. But as we do not think this exhausts the passages, we would not, even if we were a Trinitarian, explain them of the Almighty. We believe that the MAN gave shape to the universe; and, though we believe that God gave everything to the Man; yet we believe he needed this Man, to complete his works; and, therefore, that, when he says, "All things are created by him and for him" (*i. e.* in reference to him); and when he says, "He is before all things;" and when he says, " In him all things stood together" (Col. i: 16, 17),— he means, that he is the husband (house-band) of the universe; that "without him was not anything made that was made" (Jo. i: 3); that God had "chosen us in him before the foundation of the world" (Eph. i: 4); that our life was hid with him in God (Col. iii: 3); and that it was on the man alone that the promise could stand complete of eternal life "before the world began" (Titus i: 1, 2).

(4) Possibly we should stop here: but let us take another glance; and then we will finish. There is another meaning to "*dia.*" Not only does it mean *causally;* as, for example, where God says, "I will answer him by myself" (Ezek. xiv: 17); not only does it mean *normally;* as, for example, "The Lord by wisdom hath founded the earth" (Prov. iii: 19); not only does it mean *instrumentally*, in such a sense that the new Christ was necessary to the old creation; or, in other words, that God, in an age of pardons, and in an eternity of divine decrees, was really building upon Christ, and could not advance a step, except on the faith of what he was yet to be: but, once more; it means *accompanyingly;* nay more; *pregnantly.* That is; when Christ was created, all things were created. This was a bold rhetoric utterance; because Christ was created long after the heavens. But the idea, meant to be conveyed, is, for all that, apparent. "Without him was not anything made that was made." Logically, he was the precursor of the universe. That *dia* has such a meaning, we see often. "Praying often by all prayer"

(Eph. vi: 18). "Neither by the blood of goats and calves, but by his own blood." (Heb. ix: 12). "Who by the eternal Spirit offered himself" (Heb. ix: 14). "This is he who came by water and blood" (1 Jo. v: 6). The shades are very different; just as the word "Spirit," we saw, had different shades of subjectivity: but all the uses show that *dia* has singular versatility of meaning. It means, first, "by," *causal*. It means, second, "by," *normal*. It means, third, "by," *instrumental*, and instrumental in a very peculiar sense, viz., not actual, but logical, the inexistent Man being the *sine qua non* of the world's creation. And it means dia, *inclusive*.

These four all blend. The *dia* causal includes of course all that is in the Cause, viz., the wisdom and the word by which he operates. The *dia* normal refers more to the decree or plan which the unspeakable Word or self-manifesting Jehovah had before all time. The *dia* instrumental involves the instruments which that self-manifesting Word must ordain, and in the end call into being. And the *dia* inclusive is just a further thought, viz.,—when Christ was decreed, all things were decreed; and that not merely accompanyingly, as in your case or mine, but *pregnantly*. When Christ was laid down in the plan, all things were laid down. "In him all things stood together" (Col. i: 17). By him; that is, as an efflux from him,—logically all things followed. And though he was long after in time, yet John struck the key when he said, "He was before me" (Jo. i: 15); that is to say (I of course now mean the Man) was to be "head over all things to the Church (Eph. i: 22);

was to be above all "principality and power" (Eph. i: 21); was to have "all authority (power, E. V.) in heaven and in earth" (Matt. xxviii: 18); was to have "all things made with him and in reference to him" (Col. i: 16); and was, therefore, even though as a man, the first born of all things; or, as Paul expresses it, the "first born of the whole creation" (Col. i: 15).

§ 11. *The Son's Preëxistence.*

There are three ways in which the Son may be regarded; either, first, as Jehovah; or, second, as Jehovah and man; or, third, as man, apart from the Deity; that is to say, as man, aside from the other nature, but still inseparable from it, and carrying about the glories that belong to the man as the only begotten Son of the Father. Now, in all these three ways the Scriptures speak of Christ.

When, therefore, we are told, "Before Abraham was I am" (Jo. viii: 58), we have an easy course; because in that text we need only think of Jehovah. If Jesus Christ was God, we may expect him to speak of being before all time. And, therefore, when he says "I am Alpha and Omega" (Rev. i: 8), we have nothing to remember but that agreed-upon fact, "that Jesus Christ is Lord, to the glory of God the Father" (Phil. ii: 11).

But, now, by the light of what we have learned in dealing with the creation, let us remember that God was not enough to be our Maker. Forgive the irreverence. God was the Father of the Son; that is, everything that was in the Son came from the

Almighty. Therefore the Father *was* enough; for all that the Son needed God gave him. He was not only the God himself that dwelt in the Redeemer, but he made the humanity. So that all the Christ came from him; so that we cannot say, in any disparaging way, at all, that God was not sufficient for his works, and that he was not sure to execute all that he had decreed.

But we do say, that he could not execute it without Christ. God could not save without the man born in Bethlehem; and, therefore, Christ was more, in an intelligible sense, than the Almighty; for he was God in the plenitude of his substance, and he was also Man; and that Man was necessary, as a great essential of our sacrifice.

Why then should it be thought unnatural that Christ should loom up from eternity? that he should be talked of from eternity? that he should be built upon from eternity? that is to say, that nothing should be done that did not look at him; and that nothing should be planned that did not make him the central figure; so that, not yet born, he became the most familiar thought in the decree, and the most familiar object in the wide creation.

Now, immediately we can parcel out all the texts that seem to speak of a preëxistence.

1. In the first place, He did preëxist. Jesus Christ was literally God; and, therefore, he preëxisted nakedly, and in the most disentangled way (Jo. viii: 58; Heb. i: 10).

2. But, secondly, he was God and man; and there are passages that speak of him as coming down

from heaven (Jo. vi: 38); there are passages that speak of him as ascending up where he was before (Jo. iii: 13); there are passages that speak of him as emptying himself, and taking upon him the form of a servant, and becoming obedient unto death (Phil. ii: 7); and hypostatic theories seize upon this, and say, Here is no one original Jehovah without Trinity and mutuality of being, but here is a Second Person; and they conceive of these as the very strongest texts to argue an eternal Logos.

But why?

If we needed to divert our thinking, we could show that the theory of a Second Person untied these knots no more completely than the theory of One. But the reality is, that neither unties them. These beautiful sentences need more than either. The form that rises to explain them is the Theanthropos; and the second range of passages are those, which, realizing a God-man, and realizing that the man is the slenderest component of the Redeemer, talk, even when contemplating both, of the majesty of the One; and make the Great God our Saviour preëxist of course; because, though he did not pick up his humanity till the fulness of time, yet he used it, and acted upon it, from all eternity.

3. Now, there are a third class of passages, that are more rhetorical still.

Let it be remembered that the first talk nakedly of God, because God is incarnate in the Redeemer: let it be remembered that the second talk also of the Man, because God and Man are one, and yet God, being the great Fountain of the whole preëxistence, is the attribute of the nobler and constituent part of our Deliverer. But, lastly, the Man talks as though he had had immortality. That is the great phenomenon! He talks of it in a way that no Trinity could explain. He talks of it in a way not hypostatical and divine, but incarnate and human. And the question is, How could Christ, being a man, utter things before the eye of the Almighty, that seemed to imply that he, the carpenter's son, was from everlasting?

Now, it was rhetorical.

Jesus Christ, the great King of Heaven, was necessary to the universe. He did not live, till he was born; but he reigned, and was uppermost in creation, through myriads of years. "All things were made by him"; and not by him as Jehovah; and not by him as Theanthropos; but, also, by him as Man. He was before all things. Not a stone could be laid in the creation but in his name. And so familiar did he become in all time, that the whole Scripture is colored by his presence, even though he were yet to be.

Now take some of this rhetoric: "Glorify thou me with thine own self" (Jo. xvii: 5). Of course that is perfectly understandable, because Christ has just explained it: "Glorify thy Son, that thy Son also may glorify thee" (v. 1). But " glorify thou me with thine own self, with the glory that I had with thee before the world was" (v 5). The Trinitarian says, This is the Second Person; and builds at once all the mutuality of the Trinity. But let him take another text, a "Lamb slain from the foundation of the world." It is obvious that these are rhetorical liberties of the Bible: and that the Father *had* a glory; a glory that had existed from eternity; a glory in an administration based upon a Man; a glory of which that Man was an element before he was created; and a glory which, being but a Man, and being but a breath of the Almighty, and being easily commanded, and summoned up, whenever his time should come, he could be imagined as having been possessed of from everlasting, and as having had actually discounted before the foundation of the world.

"When therefore," says Augustine, "he saw that the time of his predestined glorification had fully come, that that should now happen in fact which had already happened in predestiny, he prayed saying: 'And now, O Father, glorify me, with thine own self, with the glory which I had with thee before the world was:' as though he had said, The glory which I had with thee in thy decree, it is now time that I should have with thee actually, living at thy right hand" (Augustine, Com., Jo. xvii: Tract 105, § 8).

This argument is negative. It is mightily confirmed by the testimony of such a man as Austin: but before abandoning this subject of the preëxistence, we would like to glance at something more positive. We would like to turn away from showing that certain texts do not prove the Trinity, and quote others that reject it. And I will do so in this manner. I will quote a certain text, and then ask the Trinitarian to explain it: and my object will be to show, that a downright positive sense will drift the sentence away from the preëxistence of Emmanuel.

For example, this sentence, "The first born of every creature" (Col. i: 15). If it be said, This is the eternal Logos; and if we give in to eternal generation; and if we say, This Word was derived in the beginning; and if we then seek a settled meaning by saying, This Word, being derived from eternity, preceded all creatures, and, therefore, was first derived among them all: dispensing with the hint that this is rather a gross idea, we immediately encounter other texts, which the slenderest fidelity to truth must recognize as having the same intention. Paul speaks of "the first born from the dead" (Col. i: 18). John repeats the idea (Rev. i: 5). Now, I defy any one to read from the Apostle Paul, "The first-born from the dead" (Col. i: 18), and move his finger three sentences back, and read, "The first-born of every creature" (v. 15), and say, The "first-born" in the fifteenth verse, and the "first-born" in the eighteenth verse, are heaven wide in their interpretation. The thing is impossible. And, yet, if they are not, the "first-born" in the fifteenth verse must mean the birth in Bethlehem, or else the "first born" in the eighteenth verse must mean an eternal begetting, and how, then, could that eternal begetting be a begetting from the dead?

If it be answered, They do mean differently, and it is a chance that they are thrown together: and such combinations do occur, as for example, "Answer a fool according to his folly" (Prov. xxvi: 5), and "Answer not a fool according to his folly" (v. 4), Solomon actually choosing next door positions for these utterly discrepant ideas,—I say, No exegete will be hardy enough to say so. No fair scholarship will attempt to maintain it. For, not only would one instance of just such a nature forbid, but there are other instances: not only the instance in Revelation, and not only the expression in the Psalm, fixing a time, "This day have I begotten thee" (Ps. ii: 7), but this in the Epistle to the Romans,—" For whom he did foreknow, he also did predestinate, to be conformed to the image of his Son, that he might be the first-born among many brethren" (Rom. viii: 29).

Again, I will quote another case—a text already pointed out, "The Lamb slain from the foundation of the world" (Rev. xiii: 8). Does that mean some fact that was from eternity? Did anybody ever pretend it? And if not, will the Trinitarian show what it means? And, in showing it, will he tell by what law of hermeneutic light he can read this speech of things happening in time, and save the hermeneutic strength of passages of a kindred rhetoric.

Would it be wrong to claim some positive answer to these appeals?

And, thirdly, the "Son" of the Almighty. Where did we get that word?

We have a fancy that, of all Bible names, it is the most legitimate. What a wonderful thing is theological training! The student who should be suddenly asked, Why do you say the Son of God? would answer, Because all men in all ages have used that title: or, cooling down a little, All men in Scriptural ages. And, yet, let him examine the Bible, and he will find that it is no where used except of the birth at Bethlehem.

God the Son.

Let me make one exception. Nebuchadnezzar says, "The form of the fourth is like the Son of God" (Dan. iii: 25). We turn eagerly to examine; and the first glance knocks off the article. This is positively the only passage. We have "trees of the Lord" (Ps. civ: 16); and "rivers of God" (Ps. lxv: 9); and here we have "a son of God." What can we prove by it? The monarch, in his Persian speech, says, "The form of the fourth is like a son of God." There might be bodings of a son of Abraham (Gen. iv: 1; xxii: 18; Ps. ii: 12), which might fill the world with such a speech, but how slender any influence whatever! The Psalmist says, "Kiss the Son" (Ps. ii: 12); and he says again, "Thou art my Son" (v. 7); but, of course, these are prophecies. He says, in that oft quoted announcement, "Thou art my Son: this day have I begotten thee" (v. 7), but, by the last fragment of the sentence, fixes and defines what precedes. The word "Son," like the word "Bishop," (Acts xx: 28), or like the word "Person" (Heb. i: 3), must either be borrowed, with a confession that that is not its use, (Lu. i: 35; Jo. x: 36), or this very serious adverse argument must be met—that it was no name for a preëxistent Deity.*

---

* Why should not this argument have overwhelming weight? If the filiation of the Son be eternal, and he be a Person, by that Sonship made distinct, and having subsistence in a Trinity, why is not that accented? Why is the main emphasis on what Gabriel announced? Why does not God say, and why does not he say, that he was generated before time? And why does not the birth of the Holy Ghost (Lu. i: 35) stand aside as a mere sequence in the case, and the word SON dot all the earlier annals, as chiefly belonging to a being begotten in the heavens.

Lastly, that wonderful passage in Philippians, "Who, being in the form of God, thought it not robbery to be equal with God" (Phil. ii: 6). Here I wish to ask a very different question. Here I wish to ask, Why is the Greek adjective in the neuter plural? Recollect, there is to be a Second Person; and the favorite exposition of the text is, that now he is to be described. He is "in the form of God." Unfortunate at the very first setting out! For think of it, "The same in substance," and yet "in the form"* of the Almighty! But let us go on. "Thought it not robbery to be equal with God" (v. 6). Now, of all other places in the Bible, a simple singular masculine might at once be expected. "Thought it not robbery to be an equal Person with God." Instead of that, it is neuter: and instead of the singular, it is plural. And I press a distinct answer to the difficulty that in the articulate form of speech there is no rest but in our theory. "Let this mind be in you, which was also in Christ Jesus." According to our theory, this is the great Theanthropos. "Who being in the form of God." What could be more expressive? Having the authority of God; having the name of God, so that he can stand accepted for his people; having the Spirit of God, and that in so marvellous a

---

* We believe Jesus Christ to be God, even more than our brethren: but if we believed he was a separate God, or, from eternity, a separate person in God, we would expect Paul, in so elaborate a sentence, to say something about that. We would not expect him to begin about his being "in the form of God"; just as we would not expect, in the same case, Gabriel to be telling Mary that the Holy Ghost should overshadow her, and that THEREFORE that holy thing that should be begotten, should be called the Son of God.

way, that God is in him as One Person,—it is full of significance, as he stood out upon the street " in the form " of the Almighty. And yet, there were some reserves. He was truly God. But his humanity was not truly God. And, therefore, there were certain definitions to be made. There were certain respects in which he was not Almighty. He was Almighty in emptying himself, in making himself of no reputation, in taking upon him the form of a servant, and in being found in fashion as a man; but he was not Almighty in his manhood; and there distinctions had to be made. Hence the beauty of the language, " that there should be equal respects with God " (*to einai isa*). This is no speech of an *Hypostasis*: it is no fixing of a Second Person. It is the portrait of a man: of a man claiming to be divine; of a man, actually God in the incarnation of the whole of Deity; but a man not ceasing to be man; and therefore, when stating his equality with God, exquisite in his speech, and carefully reserving respects in which he has still humanity.

But we must not make these sections too long.

§ 12. *The Angel of Jehovah.*

We think that the angel of Jehovah was a common angel, sent on the errands of the Most High. We believe so for one very strong reason, that the Apostle Paul, speaking of the incarnation of Christ, speaks in this wise, " He does not sure enough take on angels, but he does take on the seed of Abraham " (Heb. ii: 16). That scatters difficulty at a breath. He *seemed* to be actually an angel. That was his appearance. He seemed to be actually a man. But he makes a vast discrimination. He did not sure enough take on an angel; or, to make it more true to the history, any of them (plural), for he appeared in many,—but he did take on the seed of Abraham. And we are to understand that he employed angels, and that they personated him often; but that he became incarnate in the Son; and that he had, therefore, that sure-enough union, which a peculiar Greek word (*depou*) denies in the other case.

If any one asks, Is that your only passage? I say, No. Look at the last chapter of Revelation. The angel, there, rejects the worship of the Apostle (v. 9), and, yet, the next moment personates the Redeemer. "See thou do it not," he says in the ninth verse, and in the twelfth, "Behold I come quickly." This is the manner of angels. They did so at Sodom (Gen. xviii: 2, 13). They did so with Hagar (Gen. xvi: 7, 13), and Lot (Gen. xix: 1, 21); and one did so under the oak at Ophrah (Jud. vi: 11, 16, 20). Our persuasion is, that the "man" who was singled out as Jehovah, was a common angel. And if any one asks, How dare he personate God, I answer, How dare the prophets? (Œhler, Theol. O. T., § 60); or, as a most satisfying instance, how dare Moses? for most undoubtedly he says, "I will give you the rain of your land in his due season, the first rain and the latter rain" (Deut. xi: 14); and most undoubtedly he declares, "I will send grass in thy fields for thy cattle, that thou mayest eat and be full" (v 15).

The fact is, it makes the slenderest sort of difference whether it was an angel or not. If it was an angel, God appeared in him, and spoke by him, and wrought miracles by his mouth; and, moreover, gave him a human form, and wrought that miracle in the very act of sending him. If it was not an angel, still it was a human form; and it seems to make not the smallest difference. If it were the Son of God, it would not be his body; nobody pretends that. And if it were a body, God, personally in it, and representing himself by it, would be so like stretching out his arm (Deut. v: 15), as to preclude every possibility of Trinitarian demonstration.

So the matter stands, therefore. We believe that they were angels: but it is unimportant. We believe that they were angels, because the Apostle speaks so, and a distinction is drawn between the ministry of angels and the ministry of Christ (Acts vii: 53; Gal. iii: 19). We believe that they were angels, because Moses deprecated such a convoy, and pled so hard for the presence of God (Ex. xxxiii: 2, 12–15); which surely would be nothing higher than the presence of Christ. We believe that they were angels, out of deference to the straight-forwardness of speech. But grant that they were anything you please. They cannot be built into a hypostatic argumentation; for the rhetoric must remain indifferent. To send an angel, or to send an apparition, or to send a dream, or to send the Second Person in the Trinity, would be all covered under the very same miracle, and there could be no possible distinction that could breed a reasoning.

Now, one thing more.

§ 13. *The Son as Father, Son and Holy Ghost.*

Christ is distinctly called the Father (Is. ix: 6, Jo. xiv: 9). He is distinctly called the Son (Rom. i: 3). He is distinctly called the Holy Ghost (Jo. xiv: 18; 2 Cor. iii: 17). We close the chapter with that appeal to the inspired rhetoric. He is not called so, often; for that would spoil the figures; just as the "heart" is not called "mind" always or often, but only sometimes, because it is convenient to keep them separate. So the words for the Almighty are not endlessly confused; but sufficiently mixed to keep them from mystic handling.

CHAPTER IV.

GOD THE FATHER.

§ 1. *Meaning of the Name.*

PAUL says, "For this cause I bow my knees unto the Father of the Lord Jesus Christ, of whom all fatherhood in heaven and upon earth is named" (Eph. iii: 14, 15). This immediately sets a Fatherhood up which ought to have a bold and original signification. What is it? Either a fatherhood of man, or a fatherhood of God. I mean by that, the Bible is an extended revelation, and it ought very quickly to appear whether the Fatherhood that gives pattern to all the fatherhoods of the world, is a fatherhood of the Second Person of the Trinity, or a fatherhood of men; in other words, whether God was a Father from eternity, or a Father in time; the

Son, in the one case, being an Eternal Person, and the Son, in the other, being the Nazarene; the agreement in either case being that angels (Job xxxviii: 7), and men (Acts xvii: 28), are sons of the same Fatherhood, on earth and in the heavens.

Now, how could we settle such a thing? All agree that it is not debated in the Bible. Indeed, this is but one of very singular agreements. The Trinitarian agrees that his doctrine is nowhere formulated. He goes further. He says, its language is not in the Bible. He often complains of it. Calvin wished the word Trinity had never been invented. Not only is the word Trinity made up, but the word Person. *Hupostasis* is even laughably mistranslated. Not only does it never occur in the Bible to teach a Trinity; but it could not. It means a substance. The only case in which it ever occurs of the Almighty, it is mistranslated, appearing as "person"—"the express image of his person" (Heb. i: 3)—when it means "his substance;" so that the very terminology of the scheme awakens a suspicion. There is no term, Trinity. There is no dream of connecting it with anything that can be translated Person; there is no terminology of it as a faith; there is no controversy about it as of the creed; and there is no mode of settling it, except in that "Horæ Paulinæ" way, that hovers about the casualties of the expression.

Nevertheless, shut down to this, we offer this argument.

Consult a Concordance.

In the instance of a comet, do we consider the

tail as evolving the head, or the head as evolving the tail?

Turn up the word Father in a Concordance. Observe it. Where does it centre? and where does its great idea rally? It is never used of God but eight times in the Old Testament? It is never used except as of his fatherhood of man save once, and then it is prophetic of the Anointed Man, Our Saviour, the blessed Redeemer (Ps. lxxxix : 26). It is never used of an anterior Fatherhood a single time. And yet when we come to the New, the page fairly glitters with the glorious appellation.

It is never used of God's fatherhood other than as connected with a creature.

And if any body says, That is assuming everything, I speak more carefully. I do not deny that if Christ was begotten from eternity it may be *consistent* with New Testament texts. But we are speaking now of *evidence*. It will not do endlessly to empty from one mere consistency to another. We are looking for the bush where the Trinity turns upon its pursuers and rends them. I say that the Fatherhood of God is never said to be eternal. By a strange occurrence in the prophet, "The Everlasting Father" is Jesus Christ himself (Is. ix : 6). Sonship or filiation, as of eternity, would have been distinctly mentioned. It is impossible that a grand reality would have been slighted. And now, coupling-on the main argument, it is this :—That the big letters in a Concordance, scattered like the rarest stars in the Old Testament, and, when they do occur, centring, in a far off way, in the manger in Bethlehem ; and then spangling the whole heavens in the New Testament revelation,—is as near a proof as it admits, that the Fatherhood of God was not of a Logos other than as of an earth-born Son, the same in substance equal in power and glory.

§ 2. *No Name or Work Sacred to One Person.*

And the same line of remark may be made in respect to the functions of the Trinity. Controversialists are fond of saying, There is no formula, it is true; there is no controversy waged in the Bible. But, then, the facts are there. There is no gravity written in the heavens; but, then, those far off stars bear the facts of it written on their foreheads. There is no herald of the forest,—This is an oak, and, This is an ash: nor is there any schedule of the sense, proclaiming the eye or the ear: but those functionaries stand out, just as the stars shine down. And so, it may be said, Hypostases are not labelled; nor are they discussed in a doctrinal way; but there they are. And the functions of creation, redemption and sanctification mark their boundary, and, like the facts in physics, we are to collate and make their theory appear.

But, alas for the most candid seeker! there is the very difficulty. The stars wear their livery in heaven, and never change it. And so of the tree. The oak is never an ash. And, in the region of sense, the eye never listens, and the ear never looks, and the heart never breathes. But, in this most important of all doctrines as many men declare, how are we treated? There is no theory. That we must give up at once: though Paul pronounces some very strict theories as to morals (Rom. xiii: 8–10; I Cor. v: 9–11), and as to the covenants of life (Rom. v: 12–21). Moreover, there is no controversy, and there is no elenchtic discussion, to give the theory shape. The facts occur in the Bible world, like stars upon the heavens. But, now, mark the difficulty. There is no persistency in them. He who is called Creator to-day, is called Sanctifier to-morrow. There is not the abiding law, even of a well pursued emblem. The Father is called the Son, and the Son is called the Father. Both are repeatedly declared to be the Holy Ghost. And, when it comes to function, the Father is called the Redeemer, and the Holy Ghost acts as King (Acts xvi: 6, 7), and Jesus Christ is the electing Head (Jo. xiii: 18; xv: 19), and the divine Father becomes the Sanctifier of the saints (Jo. vii: 17) and, with Christ, the Quickener and the Purifier (Jo. v: 21); with nothing functional left, as the mark-manual of the Holy Ghost.

For example, Isaiah, in his glorious prophecy, says, "I Jehovah am thy Saviour, and thy Redeemer, the Mighty One of Jacob" (Is. xlix: 26; repeated lx: 16). "Thus saith Jehovah, thy Redeemer," is one of his favorite appeals (Is. xlviii: 17; liv: 8). He is spoken of as Jehovah, the Redeemer, at the very time when there is introduced, also, into the prophecy the anticipated Sacrifice (Is. xlix: 7).

In Paul we read, "The very God of peace sanctify you wholly" (1 Thess. v: 23): in Jude, "To them that are sanctified by God the Father" (Jude 1); in Paul again, "That he (Christ) might sanctify and cleanse it" (Eph. v : 26) : and in the Hebrews, " Both he that sanctifieth, and they who are sanctified, are all of One" (Heb. ii : 11).

Then, as to Election, " Ye have not chosen me, but I have chosen you" (Jo xv : 16). And, if choice of officers could be considered distinctive of the Father, then we have this sentence, " The Holy Ghost said, Separate me Barnabas and Saul to the work to which I have called them" (Acts xiii : 2); again, " take heed to the flock over the which the Holy Ghost hath made you overseers" (Acts xx : 28) : and now, once more, throwing into new confusion even such a distinctive office as the atonement, —" Feed the church of God, which he hath purchased with his own blood" (ib.).

But let us look at some of these things more distinctly.

§ 3. *The Father as Son.*

Paul says, " God was manifest in the flesh, justified in the Spirit, seen of angels, preached unto the Gentiles, believed on in the world, received up into glory" (1 Tim. iii : 16).

These texts are contraband. A theory of the Trinity is, that each of the Hypostases, in turn, is separately God.

We are driven, therefore, to texts that will say, in terms, that the Son is the Father. Now, as there could be a rhetorical prediction that the book would not so falsify its tropes as to have such a sentence, we wish to be understood as understanding the true nature of the hardship under which we live in the debate.

Still, many passages come near this very thing. Isaiah says, the child is the "Everlasting Father." Christ says, "I and my Father are one." He says, "He that hath seen me, hath seen the Father." He speaks of the Comforter coming; and then he says, "I will not leave you comfortless, *I* will come to you" (Jo. xiv: 18). And then, in another covert but unmistakable way, he cuts off from himself the possibility of having a separate Divine Hypostasis, by never mentioning it: in a long theological discussion he never realizes that. He speaks of himself, and then he speaks of his Father. He speaks of himself as weak, whenever separated from his Father (Jo. v: 19, 30). He never speaks of an Eternal Son. On the contrary, he says, "I live by the Father" (Jo. vi: 57). He says, "Of that day knoweth no man, but the Father"(Matt. xiii: 32). He says, "Father, into thy hands I commend my spirit" (Matt. xxiii: 46). He is said, "by the Eternal Spirit [to have] offered himself without spot to God" (Heb. ix: 14); not by the Eternal Logos. He never lisps of a separate Person to stand by him, and to BE he in all manner of administration. He ties himself to the Father. He says, "The Son can do nothing but what he seeth the Father do" (Jo. v: 19). We hear of "the God of our Lord Jesus Christ, the Father of glory"* (Eph. i: 17); of "eternal life which was with the Father" (1 Jo. i: 2); and evermore of just such things as we should wish to have, if what Ignatius

---

* Why not for once end that sentence—"The Eternal Son"?

says were true, that "God himself was manifested in human form for the renewal of eternal life" (Ig. p. 167; Clarks' Ed.); that "He is the mouth, altogether free, by which the Father truly spoke;" "that he is in the Father;" and that this "is all the more revealed," the more we watch the pages of revelation (Ig. p. 211).

The difficulties are futile. De Pressensé says, "It is simply impossible to conceive that the Father, in all the glory of his Godhead, can have been enshrined in Jesus, leaving as it were the throne of heaven empty" (*Her. and Chris. Doct.* p. 141). We feel helped by such a cavil. That is, God cannot be enshrined in a lily, without leaving the throne of heaven empty!

Let us pass on.

§ 4. *The Father as Spirit.*

Now, as before; we cannot expect to have much writing that shall say, "The Father is the Spirit;" for the Father is God, and the Spirit is the Breath of God, with more or less subjectivity of rhetoric. We cannot feign to ourselves the Almighty's "Arm," unless the figure is true to us, and keeps up, on occasions of its use, a good degree of tropical consistency.

But, bereft of theory, and of any illustrative polemic, and now, as it appears, of much departure from the emblem,—see what we do encounter. Jesus Christ says, "If I go not away, the Comforter will not come unto you; but, if I depart, I will send him unto you" (Jo. xvi: 7); and then he says, "Howbeit, when he, the Spirit of truth, is come, he will guide you into all truth: for he shall not speak of himself; but whatsoever he shall hear, that shall he speak; and he will show you things to come. He shall glorify me: for he shall take* of mine, and shall show it unto you" (vs. 13, 14): and then, without any intervening text, " All things that the Father hath are mine; therefore said I, that HE shall take of mine, and shall show it unto you" (v. 15). I say, It would be impossible, if there were a great underlying Trinity, that our Saviour, so grammatical in all his speeches, should drop this stitch in his discourse; and I am the more confirmed of it, because he then had done it previously.

Let us look into another chapter.

He says, "I will pray the Father, and he shall give you another Comforter, that he may abide with you forever; even the Spirit of truth; whom the world cannot receive, because it seeth him not, neither knoweth him: but ye know him; for he dwelleth with you, and shall be in you" (Jo. xiv: 16, 17): and then, without the least reverence for the Trinity, he adds, "*I* will not leave you comfortless: *I* will come to you" (v. 18); and then, a little after, " WE will come" to you (v. 23), referring to the Father.

Now, put all these things together. Remember, we have been told, " The Lord is that Spirit"(2 Cor. iii: 17). Remember we have been told, " Spirit is God" (Jo. iv: 24). Remember that it has been said,

* "Receive" E. V.) ; but the Greek is the same as in the fifteenth verse.

Christ liveth in us (Gal. ii: 20); and again, The Spirit liveth in us (1 Cor. xiii: 16); and again, God is in us of a truth (1 Cor. xiv: 25). Remember that Gabriel says, "The Holy Ghost shall come upon thee, and the power of the Highest shall overshadow thee" (Lu. i: 35), and does not stop to declare a difference. Remember that the Psalmist speaks of "the word of God" and of "the Spirit of God," and gives them the same work in the same sentence (Ps. xxxiii: 6); that Christ speaks of "the Spirit of God," in one report of his speech (Matt. xii: 28), and of "the finger of God" in another (Lu. xi: 20); that Paul speaks of the Spirit of God and of power (1 Cor. ii: 4): put all these things together; and I will insist, that, considering the decencies of the trope, there is more, rather than less, invasion of it, than its strict trope-character would idiomatically portend.

§ 5. *The Father as Jehovah.*

At this very late period in our discussion, we bring forward an idea, which might seem to have deserved to be the centralizing one in our whole investigation. It refers to the meaning of *Jehovah*. This word has excited immense attention. Among the books that have been written on this sole subject, none have been so successful, as to narrow, in the least degree, the domain of doubt. Some things have been agreed; but they have been for a long time agreed: and some things are in doubt; but they are the things that have always been in doubt; I mean within the historic period, or that compass of time that hides us from the mind of those that actually received the Pentateuch.

Now, what are the things agreed? The things agreed are, first, that Jehovah was the proper name of God; second, that the Jews were afraid to pronounce it; third, that they used instead, *Adonai*, which our translators, with a singular compliance with the superstition, have rendered "Lord"; fourth, that nothing is to be learned from the vowels in the name, because they are the vowels of *Adonai*; and, fifth, that if we could trace the consonants, that would be the most hopeful track for expounding the signification.

Now, singularly enough, the consonants are not so difficult.

Let me premise: Devas, and other Indian derivations (De Wette, I. p. 183), or, to sum it all up in a single word, all tracings of the term to languages (*Schiller's Heb. Myst.*), or to mythologic forms (*see Bib. Repos.*, No. 13), outside of the Hebrew people, have been confessedly (*Von Cölln über die Theokra*:) illusory and vain. We are thrown back upon the Hebrew: and here, strange to say, there lies nearest to our sight, and not without categorical suggestion from the Scriptures themselves, a strict and most striking signification.

Let me expound it.

Moses said, when he was commanded to go into Egypt, "Behold, when I come unto the children of Israel, and shall say unto them, The God of your fathers hath sent me unto you; and they shall say to me, What is his name? what shall I say to them?

And God said unto Moses, I AM THAT I AM" (Ex. iii: 14).

I was reading this carelessly some months ago, and suddenly there flashed up before me the future form of it. I was perfectly amazed. I seized upon the commentaries, and they recognized the fact; but languidly; and with a learned exposition how the future was more a tense for EXISTENCE than the Hebrew past. But instantly I seized the Concordance, and I could scarce find one future of the verb *to be*, that did not mean the future; and I found no cause at all for such a grammatic prepossession. I soon lit up the sentence with its own legitimately relumined lights: and, now, read the result:—"What is his name? And God said unto Moses, I SHALL BE THAT I SHALL BE: say unto the children of Israel, I SHALL BE hath sent me unto you."

Now it is but three chapters off, when there comes another discussion. "I appeared unto Abraham, unto Isaac, and unto Jacob, by the name of God Almighty; but by the name Jehovah was I not known to them" (Ex. vi: 3).

We glance at the name; and the unmistakable similarity arrests us instantly. "I SHALL BE" (Ex. iii: 14) is the first person singular future, and Jehovah is the third person singular future, of the same word, in the same exact shape, in the same unmistakable use, and, beyond all question to me now, with the same meaning.

It may be asked, Why has this been hid? It has not been altogether hid I find upon investigation (*see Bib. Repos.*, No. 13); but the reasons why it has not been intelligently accepted, seem, first, that it has not fallen into appreciative hands. The great glory of Heaven, in view of the SHALL BE when the Manhood should be taken in, had not met with appropriate favor. Let me mention further: Jehovah is an old name, older, *perhaps*, than that saying to Moses; and the verb is in an old form. The common Hebrew for the verb *to be*, is *hayah*. The older Hebrew is *havah*. The Hebrew in the speech to Moses, is the later and more common form. The Hebrew in the other would be the earlier. This is as we might expect; but then its more unaccustomed look, and the confusing of everything by the foreign vowels, have laid a veil upon the meaning. Jehovah says, "*Ehyeh esher Ehyeh.*" Jehovah's name, brought down to what was originally inspired, is "*Jehveh.*" The differences are but two: one is the later form of the verb, and the first person singular: the other is the earlier form of the verb, and the third person singular. Would that all riddles could be pressed as close! One means, I SHALL BE WHAT I SHALL BE. And the other means, HE SHALL BE, as the great name of God. And to us, in our present mind, of course, it falls as a glorious confirmation. It may be asked, Why did you not state it in the very preface? I answer, Lest it should give an air of visionariness to all the book. I would rather build upon the very commonest ideas. But now in the superstructure, having refused to allow it to be in the base of the building, it smiles upon us with peculiar beauty. God was always perfect; and, in his power, he was entire; and, in his unity, he was complete. There were no gods beside him; and, in our belief, there was no triplicity in his person. But there was one thing wanting to his work; and that was, union with humanity. Though he might be known, in rolling the stars, as God Almighty; yet when he came to the Iron Furnace, and to the region and to the period of grace, he needed more. He must prophesy there of himself, " I SHALL BE." He must be known by others as HE SHALL BE. " This is my name, and this is my remembrance," he says. And he could not build a foot of earth, or save a lost soul, but on the faith of JEHOVAH; on the bottom of that ordained Theanthropy, that was to be the base of the whole creation.

§ 6. *The Father and His Glory.*

Lit up by this view of JEHVEH, and reading some passages where the word is found, as for example, " I am HE SHALL BE; that is my name; and my glory will I not give to another" (Is. xlii: 8); or again," I, even I, am HE SHALL BE; and beside me there is no Saviour" (xliii: 11); or, "I am HE SHALL BE, your Holy One, the Creator of Israel, your King" (v. 15): hunting up some of the more salient uses of this entitlement, and then remembering, This is the Whole Jehovah, and yet Jehovah confessing that it must needs be that he come in the flesh : taking this case, —" Before me there was no God shaped, neither shall there be after me" (v. 10); and understanding that to mean, not simply that there was no God, but no administrative Father, except the SHALL BE who was to be made complete in Jesus Christ: and that, therefore, the triumph is to be understood when it was known that Jesus Christ was God (Rom. ix: 5), or, as it is expressed in the Philippians, when "every tongue should confess that the Lord is Jesus Christ" (Phil. ii: 11)—putting all these things together,—we learn to appreciate the word GLORY, which did exist from eternity, and was the essential fact with the Lord Jesus. Had he been a Hypostasis, he would have talked more of that; but the GLORY that he had with [*chez*, Fr.] the Father—that it is that fills his eye. Jesus, as man, was nothing. That he says ever (Jo. v: 19, 30; viii: 28). Jesus, as God, was everything. And, therefore, the best part of Jesus was his GLORY, viz., that which gave him a Spirit, and a righteousness, and a power, and a Kingship, and an eternity, which were the essential prerequisites of his whole sacrifice for the lost.

Listen, therefore, how that word occurs.

"Glorify me, O Father, with thine own self" (The word *para* is more like *in* than it is like "*with*." The French *chez* is almost its exact counterpart.) "with the glory that I had with (*chez*) thee before the world was" (Jo. xvii: 5); "that is, that I had as HE SHALL BE before the birth of my humanity. Being "raised up from the dead by the glory of the Father" (Rom. vi: 4). "Who being the brightness of his glory, and the express image of his substance" (Heb. i: 3). "Who gave him glory" (1 Pet. i: 21). "The light of the knowledge of the glory of God in the face of Jesus Christ" (2 Cor. iv: 6).

§ 7. *The Baptismal Formula.*

The acknowledgment having been in recent times arrived at, that the sentence in First John, "There are three that bear record in heaven, the Father, the Word, and the Holy Ghost" (1 Jo. v : 7), is an interpolation, the passage next in order in popular impressiveness is that in Matthew, "Baptizing them in the name of the Father, and of the Son, and of the Holy Ghost."

Indeed, this is so wide a formula, and has been printed on our ear, so, since infancy, that perhaps every body turns to it the soonest, when their faith in the existence of a Trinity is the least endangered.

1. Let me say, first, that this was not in such sense a formula, that the church was bound by it, or, in other words, as that we ever hear of it, afterwards, as of the practice of the Apostles. Were it a rigid formula, the argument would, of course, be greater. But, instead of that, we hear of two acts of baptism, and, in each of them, the person who was baptized, was baptized in the name of the Lord Jesus (Acts ii : 38 ; xix : 5).

2. But, secondly, it may be asked, Why a plurality of names at all? Why not say, Baptize in the name of God? To which I respond, Why not say, Believe in Christ? Christ does say, He that believeth on the Son (Jo. vi : 40), and Paul does speak of "him which believeth in Jesus" (Rom. iii : 26): why need Peter leap into a wider formula? and why does he say so carefully, " Believe in the Lord Jesus

Christ, and thou shalt be saved, and thy house?"
(Acts xvi : 31).

In fact, why does it say " name"? Why does it not say *names?* If Father, Son and Holy Ghost are hypostatically different, they may be the same in substance, and yet difference of Persons would eminently discredit the singular, " name." Our blessed Lord was God and man. As " Lord," he was the Greek for Jehovah; as " Jesus" he was Jehovah a Saviour; as Christ, he was an Anointed Man. In either of the three appellatives, there was a distinct idea; but who says that believing in the Lord Jesus Christ is anything but believing in the one Emmanuel?

3. But, it will be said; and this is by far the strongest consideration,—The Son *is* different; and, therefore, the same may be argued in respect to the Spirit. No man imagines Jesus to be different from Christ; but men do imagine the Father to be different from the Son. The Son is weak (Heb. v : 2). The Son prays (Lu. xxii : 44). The Son is man (Mar. vi : 3). The Son dies (Matt. xxvii : 50); and does what the Father could not do. Whatever may be said of the Spirit, no one denies that the Father is different from the Son: and why then, in the Baptismal Formula, do we not have a like discrepance imagined for the Spirit.

Now we have shown that the Son, as God, is one in substance with the Father. We are talking of theories now, not realities. The implication is, that we are contradicting our own theory. But let it be remembered that, on the side of God, the Father and the Son *are*, with us, but One Person. If it says,

Baptizing them in the name of the Father, the Son and the Holy Ghost, it means in the One Glorious Name (*sing.*), enthroned as the Father, enshrined as the Son, and engrafted as the Holy Ghost.

We see no difficulty. There is but one God, and Jesus Christ is the Son of God: and if any one says, Yes, but Jesus Christ, as Son, has passed into very different relations from the Father; and the argument be pressed, that the discrepance between the Father and the Son seems to imply a like mysterious discrepance between the Father and the Holy Ghost, I take issue even with that, as a fact implied in the mere enumerations of a formula.

For example, take this text,—" Your whole spirit and soul and body" (1 Thess. v: 23). Does the fact that there is a certain discrepance between the soul and body, prove, on the faith of this enumeration, that there is a like discrepance between the soul and the spirit? Or, take this text, " God, and the Lord Jesus Christ, and the elect angels" (1 Tim. v: 21). Does the fact that angels differ from God, show that there is a like discrepance between Christ and God? In fact, is there any proof in the matter? When Allen cried out, "God and the Continental Congress"; or, when the history tells us, " They feared the Lord and Samuel" (1 Sam. xii: 18); or when Isaiah says, " The Lord of Hosts is his name and thy Redeemer, the Holy One of Israel; the God of the whole earth shall he be called" (Is. liv: 5); or when Paul says, " I commend you to God, and to the word of his grace" (Acts xx: 32); or when the Chronicles say, They " worshipped God and the

King" (1 Chr. xxix : 20); or when Isaiah says, "Thus saith Jehovah, the Redeemer of Israel, and his Holy One" (Is. xlix : 7); or when Moses says, "They believed the Lord and his servant Moses" (Ex. xiv : 31); or when Paul says, "By whom we have received grace and apostleship" (Rom. 1 : 5); or when Peter and Paul both speak of " the Spirit and power" (Acts x : 38; 1 Cor. ii : 4),—I beg any one to decide, whether, in a great and sober polemic, the discrepance of these terms, or the likeness of these terms, is either to be defined or limited by the mere force of their conjugal location.

But if not, what becomes of the Baptismal Trinity?

§ 8. *The Apostolic Benediction.*

And if the Baptismal Formula is no argument, I think no one will blame me for passing by the Apostolic Benediction, as offering the same appeal, only with far feebler influence. If the form of baptism reminds each of us, at a solemn moment, of the saving relations of the Deity, the benediction actually specifies those relations. It is a sort of running comment upon the work of God. And " the grace of the Lord Jesus Christ, and the love of God, and the communion of the Holy Ghost," is a *résumé* of all that God does for man : and though, as we have all along confessed, consistent with a Trinity if there be a Trinity, yet, like all the other passages, not a proof of it. What we are looking for is positive proof. The whole course of our argument is, that the proof is illusory : that there is wonderful fencing from attack in the plea that the Trinity are the same in substance ; but that when we summon that evanescent thing a Hypostasis, the showing is not solid. There is the mere emptying of one consistency into another; without that actual proof, that would be demanded in far lower interests.

§ 9. *The Scene at Jordan.*

Witness, for example, the great insisting upon the Scene at Jordan. Turrettin goes so far as to quote, " *Abi, Ariane, ad Jordanem, et videbis Trinitatem* (Tur. Qu. xxv. § 7). Now, exhaust the proof. Jesus Christ says, "No man hath ascended up to heaven, but he that came down from heaven, even the Son of Man which is in heaven" (Jo. iii: 13). According to that, Christ has two Persons. Let us understand precisely the argument. Because the Baptized Person was down in Jordan, and the Accepting Voice was up in heaven, and the Descending Dove was hovering in the air, therefore there are three Persons in the Godhead. That is, because " truth shall spring out of the ground," it is a totally different thing, and springs from a totally different source, from the " righteousness" which looks " down from heaven" (Ps. lxxxv: 11). Because there is a " Son of Man, which is in heaven" (Jo. iii: 13), therefore he is a totally different Person from the Son of man closeted with the Ruler. Because he casts forth lightning and scatters them, therefore he is a heavenly person, and not the earthly person that shoots out arrows and destroys them (Ps. cxliv: 6). What is such argument really worth? The voice, " This is my beloved Son," was not the voice of the Almighty, but a pulsation of the air by which he miraculously revealed himself. The Descending Dove was not God, but the apparition of a bird, representing his Holy Spirit. The flesh in Jordan was not Jehovah, but the Carpenter's Son, in whom he had been pleased to become incarnate. The dramatic dislocations of the Most High are no more evincive of a Trinity, than that the Father lives in the skies, and that the Holy Ghost comes downward from the Father, and pours himself upon the head of the Lord our Advocate.

CHAPTER V.

THE TRINITY NOTHING TO THE GOSPEL.

§ 1. *What are the Gospel Ideas?*

THE shock that our creed will create is, lest it destroy the gospel ideas. This fear is not unreasonable. The denial of the Trinity in God has been like the palsy, a deadly symptom. I mean that, like the palsy, it has been so the symptom of a deadly state, that men pronounce upon it at the start, and it becomes associated, in the diagnosis of the Church, with all the deadly symptoms with which it has had incidental unity.

But this is unfair.

Moreover, the path to it has been different from ours. It has begun in laxities far down beneath it, and which travelled up to it by gradual approach. It began in Arminianism. It is a notorious fact that Geneva learned what it has learned by the track of humanitarianism and Pelagian heresy. Hence the vice of Geneva, and of all her sister cities, is that she denies the Redeemer. It is so in London. It is so in our own land. The glorious gospel of Christ perished by inanition. Now I say, There is a vast difference, in a creed that has sprung from a denial of the gospel; which has ripened in a reverence for man; which has proceeded to a dethronement of Christ; and which has come entirely to deny the Deity of our Redeemer: and one that enforces that Deity: which begins by piling every thing upon it: which makes Christ the plenary Jehovah; and which gets rid of the Trinity *a parte ante* by showing that it degrades Christ, and not *a parte post* by showing that Christ *must* be degraded, because no salvation of men and no miraculous birth is needed for the welfare of the people.

I insist that these two *geneses* of belief are totally different; and that, as the physician discovers sometimes a palsy which is as innocent as a birth; which may be incident to mere childish state; and which may be neither serious or deep,—so an anti-Trinitarian creed may be found deifying Christ, and ennobling all the doctrines of salvation.

What are these doctrines?

A denial of the Trinity, if it uphold (1) Incarnation, (2) Redemption, (3) Mediation, (4) Intercession, (5) Regeneration, (6) Justification, (7) Adoption, (8) Sanctification, (9) the Final Judgment, and (10) the Glorification of the redeemed, cannot be far astray: and if it hold them with peculiar emphasis, and make much of them, and present them in orthodox forms, surely it should be investigated twice, before it should be denounced as a damning heresy.

§ 2. *The Incarnation.*

The Trinitarian believes that the Second Person of the Trinity is incarnate in Christ. We believe that the Whole Person of our Maker is so incarnate. The Trinitarian believes that the Second Person of the Trinity must be incarnate in Christ, to give him a worth and a name adequate to our redemption. We believe that the Whole Deity is so incarnate for the same purpose, and that the Whole Deity gives the power and the worth that makes Christ a sufficient Victor for the soul's salvation.

§ 3. *Redemption*

The Trinitarian believes that Christ, being the Son of God by being united with the Eternally Begotten, lived and died as a substitute for us, both as to guilt and to punishment, and that, by force of this vicariousness, he substituted himself in our place, and, so, is ready to welcome us in his own blessed claim at the Final Judgment. We believe precisely the same thing; only, our Christ is united with God; and the Eternally Begotten, like the Eternal Sacrifice of the Mass, or like the Miraculous Wafer, seems, like the Right of Kings, or like the Divine in Baptism, to have been lightly introduced, from unresolved and uninvestigated emblematical expressions.

§ 4. *Mediation.*

To the objection, This leaves no room for Mediation: if Christ is God, and if that is carried so far as to obliterate a Trinity; and if that go to the extreme of making the One Jehovah angry with the lost, and, at the same time, die on the cross to save them,—where is the room for Mediation? and, in fact, where is the Redemption? If the same God die to please himself, where is the angry Judge? and where is the pitiful and aroused and propitiating God our Saviour?

Now, this is, in fact, two questions.

1. In the first place, Where is the Redemption?

Now, the Trinitarian himself believes that God is merciful. He believes that he instituted grace. He believes that the whole universe rang with it before time began. He believes that the Father willeth not the death of the sinner, but that all should turn and live. He believes, or else he ought to, that he taketh no pleasure in the death of him that dieth, but that all should turn and live; and, therefore, that God is no more angry than Christ (Rev. vi: 16), and no more pleased than Christ; for Christ himself is to be our Angry Judge (Jo. v: 22), and God himself was our Redeemer (Acts xx: 28), from the beginning.

He believes, therefore, that what is to be satisfied is justice, and that what is to be exercised is mercy; and he has, doubtless, often emphasized the emblem of a just judge weeping over the culprit, and, nevertheless, dooming him, in a just way, to a bitter execution.

Now, put all these things together; and put in another thing—that the Son is of one substance with the Father,—and surely there can be small complaint The Trinitarian says, The Son reconciles us to the Father; and we say, The Son reconciles us to Jehovah: and both say, Both the Father and the Son are God, and are of one mind, and have both been concerned, as the One Glorious Jehovah, in reconciling all things to himself.

2. But it will be said, Here is no Mediation. Why not?

A is a mediator between C and D. Is that the mediation of Christ? Nobody pretends it. The first Adam was under a probation; the second Adam was under a probation. Were they alike? The Apostle declares they were different (Rom. v: 12-21). There was a vicarship in either case. Was it the same? Paul carefully argues, No (vs. 15, 16). Then, listen to the lesson. All the emblems of the Bible are to be carefully regarded in their exceptions. If God is said to "repent," we are to look at it. If he is said to be "furious," we are to lay it side by side with passages that speak of him as "grieved," or as "cruel." We are to read the Bible with the usual appreciative guards. When, therefore, it says, "Now a mediator is not a mediator of one, but God is one" (Gal. iii: 20), we are to look at it as what it really is; not a pretext for a thousand glosses (see Meyer, *in loc.*), nay, for whole solid books (Bonitz, Reil, Koppe, *etc.*), but as a simple intimation that Mediatorship is an emblem in the gospel, but not a very perfect emblem, in that the Man-God is not separate from any other God, and in that the God-Man is not altogether separate from certain other men; for, as the Apostle himself argues it, "Ye are all one in Christ Jesus" (v. 28).

The difficulty of the Mediation lies here. Jesus Christ is to reconcile us to the Almighty. He is, however, himself the Almighty. He is, notwithstanding that, also man. Now, as man, he has a separate consciousness; for we learn that he did not "know" certain things that were known by his Divinity. Moreover, he had a separate will; for he says himself, "Not my will, but thine, be done" (Lu. xxii: 42). And, therefore, in this separate consciousness and will, he was "very man," as our Confession expresses it.

What trouble, therefore, in the rhetoric, if Christ, as very man, should be looked on as Mediator between Divinity and Humanity? Recollect, Person is not an inspired word. If anybody were to say, Is the Deity or Humanity of Christ a separate Person, I would decline to answer. I would say, The word is not decisive: I will tell the facts. And when I came to tell the facts, it would be thus: Christ, as having but one authority, and one forensic name, and one administrative power, is the One Almighty; but Christ, as the carpenter's son, can be looked on away from the Almighty; and, on this brother's side, I can look at him as between me and the All Wise.

§ 5. *Intercession.*

And so of Intercession.

In fact, if we look at Intercession, we will see what is the divine Mediation.

In the first place, "Intercession" is not a word of the Bible. The word in the Bible means entreaty; it means direct supplication. The idea of "*inter*" or "*between*" is not expressed in the original

(Heb. vii : 25). Intercession, therefore, as an argument from the language employed, is met already.

But, then, the very idea of prayer!

The Trinitarian says, There are three Persons in the Godhead; and, therefore, the praying of Christ to his Father is perfectly natural; and is but the entreaty of one Person to another. But discard the Trinity, and what do we behold? The Son, writhing in Gethsemane, is interceding—with himself! The argument seems to be conclusive. Either Christ is two persons; or else, if Jehovah is without triplicity, we have the preposterous scene of Jehovah wrestling with Jehovah; that is, the One Grand Divinity wrestling with itself: an idea confounding to faith, and destructive to popular impression.

But now, briefly :—Who says that Christ is not two persons? We have distinctly refused any such language. Let me explain more perfectly. The word Person is not in the Bible.* As applied to God it must be an emblem; and before I use it, I must know distinctly what it is to mean. For a man to seize it, and use it as a formidable weapon, is idle, unless he first explain what he means by it, and then it will have no force in itself, but only as a *résumé* of the facts and the principles which we must look for first in Scripture.

Accordingly, putting together a whole circle of Scripture truths, and calling it by their name, Christ is one person; and putting together another circle, he is two persons. Where is the benefit of doing either? We simply decline any such determination

* I mean, of course, as of the Almighty.

of the use. And as we are free of the word, no such word being used in revelation, we go to the principles at the very first, and refuse to pump our reasoning through this or that perfectly arbitrary expression.

Christ, as God, is one. Christ, as man, is one Christ as God-Man is two; that is to say, as our Confession expresses it, he is "very God and very man." Nevertheless Christ, as God-Man, is one. And if it were left to us to volunteer a meaning, we would say, Our meaning for Person, if any one insists on employing it, shall be in consistence with this last idea. We would say, Let Christ be a Person; and let us call him one; and let his unity be of this nature,—that, though he is unquestionably two, yet the Godhead and the Manhood have great respects of unity; first, that they are one in Court, the whole world pleading but the One Name, forensically; second, that they are one in Rule, the whole world bowing to the same sceptre; and, third, that they are one in a mysterious incarnation, the Eternal God actually entering and making himself one in Christ Jesus.

It would be these strong unities that would make me refuse to give up the word Person to any other.

But if a man insisted, and said he would use it as he pleased; that Person was not an inspired appellative, and he would say that Christ had two Persons; and if he were then to go on to explain, that Christ was entire and distinct Man, and also Eternal God; and if he were further to explain, that one person was weak and wretched, and the other glorious; that one person was buffeted and tempted, and the other the God in Heaven; if he were to say, One person shrank, and the other comforted and spoke peace,—I could not say that I like his vocabulary, but I would certainly understand it.

Nay, I could use it.

And if the Trinitarian were to press, too much, the word in the other sense, then I could enforce it; and I could say, Neither word is Scriptural; and, therefore, there are facts expounded by the one, which are not at variance with those understood by the other.

For example, prayer!

Christ was weak and wretched. Did that forbid his divine nature helping his human nature? He was ignorant. Where did he go for light? He was tempted. Who helped him? What is meant by that Eternal Spirit by which he offered himself, without spot, to God? (Heb. ix: 14). And if he could trust to that Spirit, why not pray? In other words, we believe that Christ had an entire humanity: that that humanity was equipped for every act known to man; that that humanity was distinct from the divinity; not with a hypostatic difference, leaving it the same in substance equal in power and glory, but making it different in substance, and utterly without glory (Is. xli: 24); and that this inglorious humanity could pray (Heb. v: 7) to the divinity; there being but one Jehovah; and the Father, the Son and the Holy Ghost being but One Person, subject to that complicity of state which resulted from incarnation in the blessed Jesus.

Prayer, therefore, like hunger and fasting; and like many another act; like his pain upon the cross, and like his slumber in the depths of the grave,—was an attribute of the man; and even the Trinity must so link itself with these very ideas (we admitting, of course, that the man must be supported and enforced by the God), that it can find little room for the Eternally Begotten, if the Man Christ Jesus prays directly to his Heavenly Father

§ 6. *Regeneration.*

The Trinitarian believes in a work by the Spirit, and feels confused and discomfited if we obliterate the distinction between Him and the Father. He feels as if we had denied the separateness of the operations of redemption. Yet what does the Trinitarian believe? He believes that we are born of the Spirit. So do we. He believes that that Spirit is God. So do we. All believe that we are "born of God" (Jo. v: 13). He is discomfited if ransom is confounded with the new birth. So are we discomfited. We pass on from point to point; and at last arrive at a single respect of difference. He believes that the new birth is by God, because he believes that the Spirit is one with God, "the same in substance, equal in power and glory." Can we be very far astray? He believes that the Trinity all share in each other's work. We believe that they all do the work. And our sin, if we have any, is that we deny a mysterious difference. We say that the Father new-creates (Jo. vi: 44, 65); and a beautiful fact of our system is, that it agrees with Scripture. The Scripture pays no at tention to a Trinity; and just as if the Viceroy and the Pasha and the Khedive were all the same, it speaks indifferently of either. "It is the Spirit that quickeneth" (Jo. vi: 63); and then, as though to forbid our settling upon some new-creating Hypostasis, it says, "As the Father raiseth up the dead, and quickeneth them, even so the Son quickeneth whom he will" (Jo. v: 21); and then, as though the word, God, were the prose announcement for the whole, he says, "Which were born, not of blood, nor of the will of the flesh, nor of the will of man, but of God" (Jo. i: 13).

§ 7. *Justification.*

Grant if you please the Lutheran hypothesis. The Trinitarian will declare that the angry God and the pacifying Christ *must* be two Persons. And, yet, never did a theory so break down when we come to challenge it. We ask the Trinitarian, Was God angry? He will say, Yes. We ask him, Was Christ angry? He will stop to meditate. Presently we will see that a motion is taking place in his mind. He is moving all the difference of thought and sentiment that exists between the Father and the Son away from the Incarnate Deity, and on to the man Christ Jesus. We let a long pause ensue, and then ask him, and we find that a great change has occurred. There is no such difference in the anger and in the love as he at first imagined. He finds that the Father conceived redemption (Jo. iii: 16). He finds that the Son is angry, like the Father (Matt. xxv: 41). He finds that their attitudes are shared. And when he comes to run the ploughshare of difference between the Father and the Son, he finds himself forced off on some idea of Justice. Both are trying to satisfy Justice. The Father is no more angry than the Son, both viewed as God. And if it be said, The Father was angry *at* the Son, digestion of detail soon fixes the proper relation. The Father pours out upon a Man the vials of wrath; and when we come to the constitution of that Man, the Father gives him strength (Lu. ii: 40). He is clothed with forensic dignity (Jer. xxiii: 6). Two supplements are made. He is begotten into a divine strength (Rom. i: 4); and decked with God's authority (Matt. xxviii: 18): and, when he comes to explain all this himself, he says it is his Father. "I live by the Father" (Jo. vi: 57). At any rate, God is no more angry at sin, than Christ is, as the Great Almighty (Rev. vi: 16).

The Father is said to reconcile all things to himself by Jesus Christ (2 Cor. v: 14). Where would be the propriety of this, if there were a great gospel motive for keeping separate the anger of one original Hypostasis, and the assiduity of another? Christ himself is said to reconcile all things to himself (Col. i: 21, 22); and, as though to give a parting overthrow to all idea of personalities, as between God and God, there is a text from Paul which places Jehovah precisely as we describe him—One God, apart from any distraction till he becomes Emmanuel—and then, One God tabernacling in the flesh—One God, Father Son or Spirit as we may choose our rhetoric—One God, complete in the divine decree from all eternity—but One God completed in Emmanuel, fitted by assuming flesh for the salvation of the world; building upon that en-fleshed Jehovah all creation; and not talking as though God were the Angered, and Christ were the Merciful; but laying all smooth in this crowning text, "Feed the church of God, which he hath purchased with his own blood" (Acts, xx : 28); as though "God so loved the world that he gave his only begotten Son" (Jo. iii : 16): and as though the "begotten Son" were not first an Eternally Begotten, and then a Begotten in Nazareth; but most distinctly this last alone; so that this Divine Begetter is a Father by entering, himself; by coming in, in his Whole Divinity; by pouring down, with every endowment; by making one, in the most solemn way; and by being able to say, therefore, that he reconciles all things TO HIMSELF (2 Cor. v : 18); and that he is himself the Most High, "our Redeemer," and "the Lord, our Righteousness" (Is. xlvii : 4; Jer. xxiii : 6).

§ 8. *Adoption.*

And so of Adoption. The Trinitarian is confused if we do not allow a separate Father, and a separate Spirit as a Spirit of Adoption, and a separate Son to be associated with us, that he may be the First Born among many brethren.

But singularly enough, Christ is the person that tramples upon all this. He is careful enough, where his humanity needs to be distinguished. He is very express, lest his manhood be forgotten, and lest he be too much confused with God, in his weakness (Lu. xviii : 19) and death as a sacrifice (Jo. xvii : 1);

but, where his divinity is concerned, he becomes confused at once. If Christ was discrepant from the Father, and that discrepance was not human, but began in the original Divinity, he is hard upon his people. He brings us to the brink of almost necessary error. We might have a better teacher. He does not treat us as we are, poor erring children, and keep well in hand the lines of an original triplicity; but he confounds, knowingly. He takes the most preserved peculiarities of the Father, and claims them utterly. "Ye have not chosen me, but I have chosen you, and ordained you:"

§ 9. *Judgment.*

—Nor does he stop short of the Universal Judgment. He seats himself at a bound upon the Father's throne. He speaks exactly as though he were the whole. He says, "The Father judgeth no man, but hath committed all judgment unto the Son" (Jo. v: 22): which cannot mean that the Father will not judge at all (Rom. iii: 6; 1 Pet. i: 17); but must be one of those Eastern phrases,—"They had not had sin" (Jo. xv: 22), or, "I came not to judge the world" (Jo. xii: 47): and must mean that the manhood shall be on the throne, and the plenary Jehovah shall be in judgment in him.

§ 10. *Sanctification.*

We speak, just as the Trinity does, of being sanctified by the Holy Ghost. And let it be observed, there is not one of the liturgical expressions that we do not use, if it is at all a counterpart to what is said in Scripture. We pray for the Spirit. We recognize the appointed Comforter; and think of him as coming down; and of the Holy Ghost as being poured upon us, and as dwelling in us as a perpetual temple. Moreover we believe, as others do, that he is the One God, the same in substance equal in power and glory. We only deny a triplicity. And, therefore, the Holy Ghost, who, in the Trinity, is of one substance with the Father, with us is the same Person. There can be our sole mistake. And that seems to be sanctioned by the Bible, which speaks of the lost sinner as sanctified by the Father (Jude 1), and the Son (Heb. ii: 11), and the Holy Ghost (Rom. xv: 16).

§ 11. *Glorification.*

No act can be kept distinguished. If there could be any, would it not be our being glorified? And, yet, this is constantly confused. Would it not be said, The Father shall glorify us? and should there not be fixed solid ground that must remain unaltered? But, while everything is imputed to the glory of the Father (Rom. vi: 4; xv: 7), Christ, just as if he were the Father (Jo. xiv: 10), seizes upon this last token of a distinctive Fatherhood.

Let us quote.

"Now unto him that is able to keep you from falling, and to present you faultless before the presence of his glory with exceeding joy, to the only wise God our Saviour, be glory and majesty, dominion and power, both now and ever. Amen." (Jude 24, 25). "Who shall change our vile body, that it may be fashioned like unto his glorious body, according to the working whereby he is able even to subdue all things unto himself" (Phil. iii : 21). "That he might present [the church] to himself a glorious church, not having spot or wrinkle or any such thing; but that it should be holy and without blemish" (Eph. v : 27). "Looking for that blessed hope, and the glorious appearance of our great God and Saviour, Jesus Christ" (Titus ii : 13).

29

III.

CONCLUSION.

CHAPTER I.

THE SCANDAL OF THIS BOOK.

THE geography and authorship of this book, and its relation to schools and creeds, are of course not vital to its truth, and not interesting to the general reader. But in the whole of what is called evangelical Christendom, as far as it is read at all, it will awaken a disagreeable surprise; and for three reasons.

1. In the first place, it will be thought seriously untrue. This however is the whole question in the book itself.

2. In the second place, it will be thought disagreeably presumptuous. The Trinity, to a most extraordinary degree, lies entrenched in the region of piety. Intellect has often come out against it. Locke and Newton and Milton, whatever their pious claims, are chiefly remarkable in the region of the mind. A man may embolden himself in heresy by saying, Hume is with me, or Boyle is with me, or Shaftesbury thinks as I do; but it is a ghastly comfort; because there are the assurances of Scripture that this worldly intellect is specially to be put to shame

Locke certainly denied the Trinity. So did Newton. So did Milton. Moreover they were not infidels; and, what is far more interesting, they were professed worshippers of Christ. But, perhaps, Gamaliel was a good man. We stand in awe, rather, of intellect, when it comes to knocking away the pins of what have been thought great truths of the gospel.

Isaac Watts denied the Trinity. Here we have piety and rare gifts besides. And though there can be no question of the fact, and, after all the efforts of his biographers, it cannot be made out that it was the faltering of his stricken faculties, or the aberration of a crazy mind; though there are sane letters telling why he could not alter his hymns, and how the property in them had passed, and was entirely out of his control, and had been so for thirty years; though there can be no earthly doubt that he who wrote

"Alas! and did my Saviour bleed?"

lived, in the entire ripening of his powers, to deny and disown the separate personality in God, yet, alas! he denied and disowned the Deity of his Redeemer. The shelter is but a forlorn one. Locke and Newton and Milton did the same.

On the whole, it is a pleasant thing, when we find our creed not in the Bible, to say, Newton thought so, and Locke and Milton; and they thought so in their maturest and most pious period: and it is an assuring thing to discover Watts thought so; and in all the aroma of earnest faith, wrote so to the world, just as he was ascending to his heavenly Father: yet, alas! this is but a poor sort of prop. In the first place, These are but a few. In the second place, These are not specimen men, but men of advanced thought; and, in the main, of very enthusiastic ideas. In the third place, They became Arian, or something worse. And though we say, How many more would join them if they were shown, as we have tried to do, how Christ can be preserved, and yet there be a denial of the Trinity,—still, all this remains to be proved. There is a scandalous look of presumption in just such a book as this. Our own feelings, but a few years ago, would have turned from it with disgust. The only excuse for it must be, a very profound conviction. And though it is right to say, Locke and Newton and Milton parry it a little, and Watts spreads over it the mantle of excuse; and though each of these could have dissected away the Trinity and kept Christ, if they had observed the exegesis followed in the preceding plan; yet all this goes for very little. Unless the Trinity, like the Real Presence, has come, in the counsels of eternity, to its period of decline, woe worth the present enterprise, and woe worth the reckoning of any man, who kindles the bale-fires of death in face of the noon-day light of a blessed revelation.

3. In the third place, What doctrine will come next? This is, perhaps, of all others, the most reasonable misgiving of the church. The sin of Presbyterianism has been to deny Emmanuel. Here its plague has begun. It has not been in an overhonored sacrament: the fall of Genevism has begun in an underhonored Lord and Divine Sacrifice.

So the church is fully warned.

And I cannot but emphatically agree, that a finger raised against the Trinity ought to be watched like a match in the magazine of a Monitor. There should be no trifling here. But, beyond all question, there is to be this admission—that error is to be no shelter for the truth. Our Lord said, "Let both grow to the harvest." But he uttered that of men, not of doctrines. The man that teaches that weeds must shelter the crop, debauches his religion. The church, in our day, is not a weakling, such that she cannot bear the most fruitful investigations: and if she were, she would have no right to withhold them. The simple point is, Is there a Trinity? If there is, no weapon formed against it will prosper. If there be not, it is a shameful disrespect to the Master to be sheltering him, as the glorious God, behind a baseless dogma of a Pagan Platonism.

CHAPTER II.

THE BENEFIT OF THIS BOOK

1. ALL truth is of necessary value. If the Trinity is not a fact, it clogs and clouds the actual doctrines of the gospel.

2 The Trinity is hard to teach. We are holding out our hand to distant and stupid Pagans. Men's lives are going into the scheme; and patient women are withering under unwholesome skies. The dogma of the Trinity costs missionary life; for, all the time spent in propounding it, if it is false, or defending it, if it be not defensible, is like what Paul speaks

of as beating the air. It is keeping back the lost from mercy, and loading the principia of grace with what Paul calls " unsanctioned fables" (1 Tim. iv: 7).

3. Third, it almost prohibits certain entrances among the perishing.

Oh, if Mohammed had not found the Trinity in Damascus! if that pale-faced youth had not encountered, in his aroused conscientious frame, the *Hypostasis* of the Bishops! if the Old Man of the Sea had not jumped on Sinbad on his first setting out upon the deep,—who can tell what young Mohammed might not have been formed to be?

At any rate, everybody will admit, that, if the Trinity be a mistaken heresy, it will give us new life, to unseat it: and that Southward among the African Lakes, and Eastward among other Mussulmans; that among the Unitarians of our own land, and among Jews all over the world,—the doctrine of One Great God, and he incarnate in the One Man Our Saviour, would give us a new power to work, and give us altogether a noble form in which to cast the enterprise of the gospel.

THE END.

Made in the USA
Middletown, DE
28 October 2016